Learning to be Literate

Insights from research for policy and practice

Margaret M Clark

Glendale Education Birmingham

First edition published 2014

by Glendale Education: 61 Jacoby Place, Priory Road,

Birmingham B5 7UW

ISBN 978-0-9928931-0-1

Printed in England and distributed by Witley Press Ltd, 24-26 Greevegate, Hunstanton, Norfolk, PE36 6AD

Contents

List of Figures

Preface

With the exception of chapters 1 and 21, the chapters in this book are based on adaptations of previous publications on research by this author. They have been selected because of their continuing relevance for policy and practice, or because such insights had been ignored by policy makers, and on occasion by practitioners. There are five sections with different themes. All four chapters in the first section relate to research prior to 1990, were originally presented at conferences in different parts of the world and later appeared in written form in the proceedings. The first chapter in Section II was also presented at a conference, the remaining four chapters illustrate ways in which, based on research, creative environments can act as a stimulus for young children learning to read. Here the researcher becomes a practitioner, hopefully providing new research-based insights.

In Section III attention turns to literacy policies in England, Wales and Scotland as they diverged following the first national curriculum in England and Wales in 1988. Section IV, concerns *politics* and its impact on recent literacy policy in the years 2006 to 2014 in England, where synthetic phonics was adopted as the method of teaching reading. The evidence base for this policy, its implications for schools and the costs are explored in five chapters. In the final chapter in this section the debate is widened to include evidence from other countries on the impact of commercialism on the literacy policies adopted by politicians. Questions are raised as to whose evidence should count in determining literacy policies.

Section V chapter 19 reveals the dangers of basing, or modifying literacy policy on international surveys, even those as large-scale and well-planned as PIRLS and PISA. Here the focus is on sampling issues rather than on the results of a particular survey; thus the analysis has wide implications. Chapter 20 is based on a seminar presentation with a wide remit, covering adult literacy and developments in Europe. In chapter 21 insights on literacy from research are backed with illustrations from children and adults. Finally, the influence of orthographies on literacy development is considered.

Acknowledgements

I am grateful to all those who have informed, stimulated and inspired me:

Researchers whose publications I have studied, many of whom I have been fortunate enough to meet;

Students, many themselves practitioners, with whom I have shared ideas and who have provided me with many examples of creative illustrations from children;

Colleagues in the settings in which I have worked who have supported me in my ventures, either formally as researchers, or informally by sharing their thoughts and widening my horizons;

Children of all ages and their parents, who have challenged me by their ability and creativity.

I am grateful to all these people, too many to name, friends and colleagues who have encouraged me throughout this new adventure into self-publishing. I could not have succeeded in bringing this to fruition without the assistance and technical ability of the following:

Bob Ridge-Stearn, Head of e-Learning at Newman University and Samantha Bryant, for their crucial technical support and patience with my naïve questions;

Sarah Baxter of The Society of Authors for her advice on self-publishing;

Chris Witley of Witley Press Ltd for his speedy response to my many queries and his company's efficient treatment of my work.

While this new venture has on occasion been stressful, it has also been a challenge, and fun. Furthermore, I can now claim not only to have had this book printed speedily, to my specifications, but also to be a publisher!

Margaret M Clark   March 2014

Chapter 1
Introduction

Rationale for the book

My publications on literacy over the years 1967 to 2014 have included conference papers, articles, chapters in books, research reports and books, either as author or editor. In making my choice of what to include in this book I have selected those publications that still have relevance today, highlighting evidence from research or lessons we could have learnt, many ignored by those making policy decisions. In some instances where I had competing publications, I selected those that most succinctly focused on my chosen themes. Where I do not hold the copyright I sought permission from the copyright holder to publish adapted and edited versions of the previous publications; this is indicated in the introduction to the various sections of the book. Chapters 1 and 21 have been written specially for this book.

My interest in literacy developed during my time as a primary school teacher, and later as a lecturer in a college of education. Having joined the United Kingdom Reading Association in 1964 I founded the West of Scotland Reading Association the following year. Together with members of the newly founded local association I undertook a study in schools in the Glasgow area of an experimental television series for backward readers, following a presentation by the producer about the programme at our first meeting. My first conference paper for UKRA in 1966 was a report of that study. I decided not to include it in this book, although it is an example of a collaborative study involving members of a newly founded association, and some of the lessons we learnt are still relevant. However, the published version is available in two UKRA publications in 1967 and 1972 (see reference list at the end of the book).

I was president of UKRA in 1972 and have included a shortened version of my presidential address (published in 1973). Between 1966 and 1991 I gave papers on literacy at a number of UKRA annual conferences. I have also given papers at conferences and seminars in a number of other countries, most subsequently published. Among those I have selected to adapt for inclusion here are those from Australia, Canada and Sweden.

My first major research on reading was published in 1970, a community study of children with reading difficulties. In 1976 my second major study was published, a contrasting series of case studies of young children who were already reading with understanding when they started school at five years of age. In 1979, on moving to Birmingham, I continued to lecture and in parallel to undertake research, encouraging my students, many of them practitioners, to undertake their own researches or collaborate in mine. As a consequence of a request from a director of education in early 1970s to undertake research in his newly opened nursery schools, I became interested in the fascinating field of preschool children's differential awareness of the elements of printed language. I was able to share insights from case studies, my own and internationally known researchers, with my students. I have included reference to these developments as currently there seems to be insufficient recognition given to the wide differences in concepts of print between children on entry to school, even where none of them can yet read.

Developing the book

Having made my selection, the original publications were either scanned, or if possible, where a word document was available, that was used. None of the chapters contain the original publication exactly as it appeared originally. Some have been shortened, either because of the length of the original or because of overlap with other chapters. Editorial changes have been made to achieve consistency in referencing; in some instances wording has been improved. Changes have been kept to a minimum, and where comments or references have been added this is clearly indicated. Thus it is hoped that the book records changes in emphasis in research over time, insights we could have gained and lessons we should have learnt. Hopefully it might put to rest some myths, including those perpetuated by successive governments, where they fly in the face of a wealth of research evidence.

Outline of the book

The book is in five sections and within each section and chapter the scene is set briefly to enable readers, should they wish, to focus on specific chapters or sections. Chapters 1 and 21 were written for this publication.

The four chapters in Section I are based on written versions of papers I presented either at conferences or seminars, with the theme `Insights from Literacy Research from 1960s to 1980s`. Chapter 2 is a shortened version of my presidential address from 1972. I have omitted my comparison of standards of literacy between Scotland, where evidence was of rising standards, and England where at that time it was claimed they were falling, also the discussion of a newly published Edinburgh Reading Test. Chapter 3 is a shortened version of a paper I was invited to give in 1973 at a Social Science Research Council seminar on `Problems of Language and Reading` where papers were also given by James Britton. Jerome Bruner, Michael Halliday and H. H. Speitel. Among those present and taking part in the discussion were leading researchers including Joan Tough, Margaret Donaldson, Marie Clay, Jessie Reid, John Merritt and Basil Bernstein, who chaired the seminar.

Chapter 4 compares the evidence from my community study of children with reading difficulties and my case studies of children who could read with understanding on entry to school at five years of age. This chapter is based on a paper delivered in Australia in 1981. In chapter 5 I consider insights from a further analysis of my study of young fluent readers undertaken for a seminar in Canada on literacy, convened by Frank Smith in 1983. In addition to Frank Smith, papers were given among others by Yetta Goodman, Jerome Bruner, Glenda Bissex and Emelia Ferreiro, all of whom were involved in the discussions. The papers were published in 1984 in *Awakening to Literacy* edited by H. Goelman, A. Oberg and F. Smith.

In Section II attention turns to ways that research can provide insights for practice, in short, How to Help Young Literacy Learners.

Chapter 6 is based on a paper given in Lund in Sweden in 1987 on creative contexts for literacy learning, at a conference on the Study of Child Language. It was published in *Children's Creative Communication,* Ragnhild Söderberg (ed) in 1988.

Chapter 7 is a tribute to Marie Clay whose research into the importance of sensitive observation of young children's early encounters with print and her development of Reading Recovery I studied both from her publications and during a visit to New Zealand. The remaining chapters in this section, chapters 8, 9 and 10 are based on my practical work with young children published between 1994 and 2013. I worked as a volunteer in an inner city school in Birmingham, gave workshops to groups of teachers and encouraged my students to collect examples of young children's earliest encounters with print. Illustrations from some of these children are to be found in chapter 8. The focus in chapter 9 is on ways of helping children to learn the hundred key words that account for about 50% of the total words in written English. This is based on an article published in *Reading News.*

Over the years 1986 to 1988 I worked with a colleague, Wendy Dewhirst, as a consultant to a Granada television series, *Time for a Story.* We gave advice on the programmes and developed teachers' booklets with suggestions for further activities based on the programmes. Twenty-eight stories were written by well-known children's authors specifically for the series, each was the focus for one of the programmes for children aged four to six years of age. Little books with the stories and illustrations from the programmes were available. I subsequently used recordings of some of these programmes and also some of the story books to stimulate young children's writing. The reciprocal relationship between reading and writing is the theme in chapter 10, with examples from children's writing and illustrations based on these stories.

In Section III attention turns to developments in government policy on literacy over the years 1988 to 1995, in England within The National Curriculum and in Scotland during the development of the National Guidelines. In chapter 11, the National Curriculum and related assessments following The Education Reform Act in 1988 in England and Wales, are discussed. This is based on extracts from a publication of mine in 1995 entitled, *Language, Learning and the Urban Child.* The developments in Scotland over the same period were very different, with National Guidelines 5-14 based on reports of working parties with representatives of the teaching profession, advisers and college lecturers playing an important part. Chapter 12 is based on chapter 3, `Developments in primary education in Scotland`, in *Education in Scotland: policy and practice from pre-school to secondary*, editors M. M. Clark and P. Munn (1997).That book traces developments up to devolution in 1997. From these two chapters it can be seen that policies in England and Scotland were already very different even before devolution.

In Section IV the theme of policy is continued, with the focus on politics, following claims made by government for one best method for teaching reading, namely synthetic phonics. These can be traced back in England to the Rose Report in 2006. All six chapters in this section are from articles published in the *Education Journal* between 2006 and 2014. They are included here with permission of the editor of the journal. Chapter 13 is a critique of the Rose Report, followed in chapter 14 by an analysis of research evidence for claims for one best method of teaching reading between 1966 and 2014. Not only did the government in England claim that synthetic phonics was indeed the best method, and that it was backed by research, but it devised a phonics check to be administered to all children in Year 1, aged from five to six years of age. This test of 40 words, half pseudo words, with a pass mark of 32 was first administered in 2012. Its development, results and effects after the first and second years of its administration, 2012 and 2013 are discussed in chapters 15 and 17. Brief reference is made to the recently released changes in the check for 2014. In chapter 16 the results of the first interim report from the National Foundation for Educational Research, commissioned by the Department for Education, are analysed.

In chapter 18 some of the costs of the phonics check and of the commercial materials and training courses recommended by the government are reported. This information was obtained under the Freedom of Information Act. In the second part of that chapter the discussion is widened with evidence from a recently published book, *Whose Knowledge Counts in Government Literacy Policies?* K. S. Goodman, R. C. Calfee and Y. M. Goodman (eds) (2014). It appears that commercial interests are gaining an increasingly powerful place in government policies in many parts of the world, including, The United States, Germany, France and also in many developing countries. The theme has now become `Whose Knowledge Counts in Literacy Policies?` A disquieting picture is painted of the power wielded by large commercial organisations to influence government literacy policies, often falsely claiming a research basis for the policy.

Section V has two chapters, the first based on an analysis of PIRLS, an international comparison between countries based on assessment of children aged about ten years of age in 35 countries. Studies such as PIRLS, and PISA on fifteen year olds, often gain publicity in the media and influence government literacy policies, with politicians either preening themselves or impetuously making major changes should their country`s ranking appear to be falling. In chapter 19, based on an article in the *Education Journal*, the focus is on the sampling and limitations of international studies such as PIRLS, even when such studies are carefully planned and rigorously executed. Since 2003 when these results were published there have been further studies. There are still lessons from this analysis, as some of the limitations identified are inevitable in such large scale studies with data from so many countries. Chapter 20 is based on a paper delivered in Brussels, then published in 2012 as chapter 5 `Literacies in and for a changing world` in *Improving the Quality of Childhood in Europe,* C. Clouder, B. Heyes, M. Matthes and P. Sullivan (eds). Here the discussion is widened, and includes developments in Europe and adult illiteracy.

In chapter 21, the characteristics of written language, and in particular the complexities of the English language are explored further. The focus in this book has been mainly on learning to read and write in English, as has been much research. A recent publication on Orthographies and Literacy widens the topic to include other languages and orthographies.

Section I
Insights from Literacy Research: 1960s to 1980s

The first two chapters are based on written versions of papers presented in 1972 and 1973; thus, the references are from researches published between 1960 and 1973; yet the issues discussed still have relevance today. Reference was made at both presentations to my then ongoing study of children who could read when they started school at five years of age, published in 1976 as *Young Fluent Readers: what can they teach us?*

Chapter 2 is a shortened version of the presidential address I delivered at the United Kingdom Reading Association conference in Glasgow, `Reading and Related Skills`, published in the proceedings in 1973. This is published with permission from UKLA, the copyright holder.

Chapter 3 is a shortened version of a paper delivered at an SSRC seminar in Edinburgh. Selected points from the discussion are also included. Those delivering papers and taking part in the discussions included key researchers into language and literacy. The seminar papers and discussions were published in 1975 in *Problems in Language and Learning* edited by R. Davies This amended version of my paper is published here with permission from the copyright holder ESRC.

The other two chapters are also based on written versions of oral presentations. The first presentation was in Australia in 1981 and the second in Canada in 1983. They draw on two of my researches, the first a community study, *Reading Difficulties in Schools* published in 1970; the second case studies of children who could read with understanding when they started school at five years of age. This was published in 1976 as *Young Fluent Readers: how can they help us?*

Chapter 4 is an edited version of a paper in *Reading, Writing and Multiculturalism*, 1982, D. Burns, A. Campbell and R. Jones (eds). Adelaide: Australian Reading Association: 96-103, a written version of a plenary session paper given at The Australian Reading Association

Conference in Canberra in 1981. There are comparisons of these studies in other publications, in 1975, 1984 and 1989 (see reference list). I selected this version from the Australian conference as it covers a wider range of the issues. It provides a brief outline of the two studies and a discussion of the lessons we can learn from a comparison of the relative strengths and weaknesses of the two groups. There is also a brief critique of the limitations of educational research. This chapter is published with permission from the copyright holder, the Australian Literacy Educators' Association.

Chapter 5 includes further analysis of the study of young fluent readers, prepared for a seminar in Canada in 1983 convened by Frank Smith. In addition to Frank Smith, papers were given by a number of internationally known researchers, who also took part in the discussions. These included Yetta Goodman, Glenda Bissex, Jerome Bruner and Emelia Ferreiro. The seminar papers were published in 1984 in *Awakening to Literacy,* H. Goelman, A. Oberg and F. Smith (eds). This adaptation is published with permission from the copyright holder, The University of Victoria.

Chapter 2

Reading and Related Skills: lessons from early 1970s

This is a shortened and edited version of my presidential address at the United Kingdom Reading Association Conference in 1972, published in 1973 in *Reading and Related Skills,* M. M. Clark and A. Milne (eds).

Background

It is valuable to be aware of the outlook and the problems of those from other countries and disciplines; otherwise we are in danger of failing to appreciate the extensive educational possibilities which our own school system denies us.

Different perspectives on reading

As *teachers*, we tend to look for solutions within the existing framework of the classroom and school. In Britain, we assume children should begin school at five years of age, or earlier, and stay until sixteen (or later). We assume that they should be in school all day and that a shortened school day is deprivation. Within schools one of our objectives is that all our children will be reading by the age of seven, otherwise they will be at a permanent disadvantage. To what extent is any disadvantage an inevitable consequence, or merely the result of our particular school approach to education and school organization, or our failure to cater for children's varied needs and individual rates of development? While seeking our short-term solutions within the present educational system, we should look beyond that in our evaluation of its long-term effectiveness.

We should look to other countries to see whether we are perhaps too much concerned with amount of time spent in school and too little concerned with the quality of the provision. We should look to other agencies to see whether we perhaps overvalue the role of the teacher in education and underestimate the crucial role played by many parents. We may also overstress the part played by educationally accepted books and materials in the teaching of reading and undervalue the potential of other materials, including environmental print and the media in learning to read.

If as *college of education lecturers* we meet only others with a similar background, we may well seek to extend the initial training of teachers, claiming that only then can the training be adequate in imparting all the knowledge that the students require, forgetting, perhaps that some aspects of competence can most successfully be taught in-service; some can be taught in no other way. Perhaps we attempt to pack too much into pre-service training. Were we, in teaching, dealing with a body of facts to be acquired by the intending teacher and passed on to the expectant young child, perhaps there might be justification for such a course. Colleges can help by encouraging students towards a critical appraisal of new developments and an analysis of existing practices, rather than by encouraging uncritical acceptance of an existing body of knowledge, no matter how extensive.

As *psychologists* we need, at least as much as anyone, to discuss with others developments in the teaching of reading. Psychologists, by the nature of their professional involvement, tend to be preoccupied with failures. Apart from studies of the relative effectiveness of various competing methods or media as the best approach to the initial teaching of reading, psychological research has often concentrated on children who have failed in reading, their intelligence, language and home background, or more recently the school background. Other important factors contributing to success in reading may then not have been appreciated.

As *researchers* we should consider the characteristics of successful readers worthy of investigation to illuminate our understanding of reading as a form of communication. Such studies should, in addition, lead us to a more accurate perception of the role of various deficits as causal factors in reading failure. We may find indeed that some fluent readers are highly successful in spite of such disabilities.

A topic that for many years attracted a great deal of attention was the measurement of the percentages of non-readers at seven, eleven or fifteen years of age, with comparisons of these in different schools, areas or countries, or at different times. These studies have aroused controversy as to whether the percentages are different now from previously, with more failures, by some blamed on progressive methods. This dichotomy of those who can and those who cannot read has on occasion carried with it the implicit assumption that teaching children to read is an all or none process; the concern of the teachers in the early part of the school, with subsequent teachers mainly involved in dealing with those with whom the initial teaching has failed.

Comparative studies of standards of children at seven years of age may be more dangerous than valuable, when averages within an area or country are treated in isolation, as so often happens. Does it matter if some children cannot read at seven? Are they not reading because of a conscious policy to delay reading instruction and extend the period of oral communication, or are they failing in spite of a conscious policy of instruction? There is a place and an important place for assessment in the teaching of reading, provided it leads to monitoring of progress and action. Some teachers` distrust of tests is unfortunate but understandable. All children identified as failing at seven years of age would not necessarily require specialist treatment but the schools, with the aid of diagnostic tests could be alerted to their existence. Their progress could then be monitored from an early age and modifications made to enable them to access the full curriculum.

The early start in the teaching of reading, the systematic instructional techniques and the tendency towards a more phonically based approach could help children to perform well on a task which involves word identification from a selection of alternatives. Such a test while designed for, and indeed useful for, identifying children who have failed to make a start in reading at the end of the infant stage, is scarcely adequate as a measure of good reading. Learning to read should not be regarded as a hierarchy of skills from lower to higher order, but as a developmental language process. The approaches in the initial stages will colour the children's motivation and their perception of reading as a purposeful and valuable activity. On completing their schooling children should not only be able to read with comprehension for a variety of purposes, but also be motivated to read.

Perhaps as *educationists* we are too ready to accept credit for the successes and to attribute the failures to the parents. We can never know how many of the children who read critically and purposefully after attending school would have read effectively had they been at home! The term compensatory education is unfortunate in its implied condemnation of the home. We perhaps overvalue the specialist and undervalue the contribution of the parents. Parents are being made to feel less and less adequate, and in some settings have little more than a peripheral role.

Children and beginning to read

Just as we are in danger of undervaluing the role of the parents, so also we are in danger of failing to appreciate the characteristics which the child brings to the reading task. To quote Smith (1971):

> Two things are perhaps surprising about the skills and knowledge that a child brings with him when he is about to learn to read: the sheer quantity and complexity of his ability, and the small credit that is usually given. (223)

Reading readiness as a concept with its emphasis on the inadequacies of the child, tends to reassure insecure teachers that the failures were not theirs but the child's. There must be few characteristics measured in any test of reading readiness which are absolute barriers to learning to read. Some may make a particular technique or group situation inappropriate. The child with poor auditory discrimination may find it more difficult to learn by a phonically based approach, particularly if the classroom is noisy. Children with poor visual discrimination may have their difficulties increased by a look-say approach, particularly if the teacher's writing is not clear. The child with limited grasp of language may have problems if the teacher's explanations are predominantly verbal, or unnecessarily complex. Some recent studies of children's concept formation appeared to reinforce assumptions about the children's inadequacies. However, one must distinguish between a child's ability to solve a problem and their ability to verbalize a solution.

It is salutary to bear in mind there are children who might have failed some tests of reading readiness who may by three or four years of age already be fluent readers. Readiness of the school for the child should now be given as much attention as readiness of the child for the school. In a study of children who were already fluent readers when they started school, I was impressed by a number of aspects of their fluent reading. These might not have occurred to me had I confined my attention only to children who had learned to read in the school group situation. One aspect that worried me considerably was the parents' embarrassment that they had sent their child to school able to read. Why should we make parents feel guilty if their child comes to school able to read, and ashamed if they come not ready to read?

Not all children in my study were highly intelligent; not all their parents were professionals. Indeed, not all had a range of interesting and stimulating children's books for their first experiences of printed material and certainly few had any structured reading scheme. Unlikely materials like car numbers, the daily newspaper, the Radio Times, an old pack of lexicon cards and even television advertisements acted as a stimulus to these children, and could do to other children. One important common factor for these children seems to have been an interested adult. One characteristic of these children was their awareness of what they could and could do. This study was later published as *Young Fluent Readers: what can they teach us?* (Clark,1976).

Children, when they start school, do not have to be taught language, but the written representation of language. They do not have to be taught to look, they have to be taught the significant characteristics of print. They need to know enough, not all, about the letters. Fluent reading does not necessitate a minute analysis of each aspect of each letter or word but only sufficient to extract meaning from the printed page. Frank Smith's insights made an impact, and made many reappraise their ideas on the crucial elements in reading instruction. As he stated in 1971 in *Understanding Reading:*

> A clearer understanding of what the skilled readers can do, and of what the beginning reader is trying to do, is far more important for the reading teacher than any revision of instructional materials. (230)

> The `decoding` that the skilled reader performs is not to transform visual symbols into sound, which is a widely held conventional view of what reading is about, but to transform the visual representation of language into meaning. (222)

A large number of interrelated skills developed over a period of years are necessary for reading. Ability to recall nonsense syllables does not differentiate good and poor readers (Merritt, 1970). A willingness to make mistakes may be part of the process of learning to read, and guessing may only be bad for a child if it is based on wrong cues. It may be a stage in the development of linguistic competence leading to fluent reading. The child has to discover the distinctive features of print, of words and of letters. The teacher must be aware of the significance of the various characteristics of language and of print. For example a and I are both letters and words; I and ! may look similar, but have different functions in written language. When, for example, we talk of two letters being 'the same' or 'different', what do we mean? As Reid (1960) indicated, many five-year-old children have limited appreciation of the difference between a letter, a word and a number.

The child must learn by response and by feedback from the teacher or another adult. This appears to have been one of the roles that the parents played for the precocious readers referred to earlier. Many of these children initiated the questioning; the parents confirmed the hunch or suggested an alternative when the child could not otherwise make sense of the reading material. Some studies of children's concept formation seem to have reinforced feelings of the children's inadequacies. One must, however, distinguish between children`s ability to solve a problem from their ability to verbalize the solution. Even many of the fluent readers in my study at five years of age could not verbalize the concepts, but they certainly had some appreciation of their function. As pointed out by Brandis and Henderson (1970), let us not underestimate children's understanding because of their inability to describe their solution.

Reading and writing, a reciprocal relationship

Just as purpose, and purpose seen by the child, is important as a motivating force in learning to read, so purpose in writing is important in written communication. This gives point to the teaching of handwriting and spelling as aspects of written communication, as tools. Though spelling can be caught by some, it can also be taught to the others, as stated by Peters (1967). This is most effective when the instruction is systematically organized, taking into account the linguistic probabilities of the English language, and the child's needs within their written communication for the words being taught.

If we wish to develop literacy in all children, then we must proceed developmentally from oral communication for a purpose in a wide range of contexts to an integrated approach to reading and writing. If one considers the extent to which children, even from so-called deprived homes, are bombarded with speech, one appreciates that their difficulties may arise not from lack of speech, but rather lack of communication. No language programme will succeed in which the children are the passive recipients of the teacher's speech, no matter how stimulating and varied, unless this leads in turn to wide and varied participation by the children themselves. As Merritt (1970) stated:

> What could be less motivating than the repeated setting down of the obvious for the already well-informed... the critical feature in developing communication skills (is) the opportunity to communicate with an army of different recipients on a variety of subjects in a variety of contexts.

An educated person may be defined as one who has acquired the ability to listen thoughtfully, to speak effectively, to read critically and to write creatively. Are these realistic aims for the teaching of reading and the related skills, if so for only a chosen few, or for all but a small minority? Our professional competence will determine the answer.

References

Brandis, W. and Henderson, D. (1970) *Social Class, Language and Communication.* London: Routledge and Kegan Paul.

Clark, M. M. (1976) *Young Fluent Readers: what can they teach us?* London: Heinemann Educational. NB added later.

Merritt, J. (1970) `Teaching reading in junior and secondary schools`. *Teaching Reading: Ace Forum 4.* London: Ginn.

Peters, M. L. (1967) *Spelling: caught or taught?* London: Routledge and Kegan Paul.

Reid, J. F. (1960) `Learning to think about reading`, *Educational Research*, 9,1: 56-62.

Smith, F. (1971) *Understanding Reading: a psycholinguistic analysis of reading and learning to read.* New York: Holt, Rinehart and Winston.

Chapter 3
Language and Reading: insights from early research

This is an edited, shortened version of `Language and reading: research trends`, chapter 4 in *Problems of Language and Learning*, A. Davies (ed) 1975, the written version of a paper I delivered at a seminar sponsored by SSRC in Edinburgh in 1973.

Background

For many years research into learning to read concentrated mainly on negative aspects, levels of illiteracy, causes of failure and remedial techniques. This was unfortunate, because of the wide range of aspects left unstudied, and the danger of erroneous conclusions drawn from those with difficulties. That emphasis could lead to a mistaken evaluation of the significance of certain disabilities and to a limited conception of the skill defined as reading.

Readiness and reading

Disappointingly little of value has been uncovered by studies of reading readiness based on tests (Downing and Thackray, 1971). As early as 1963 Krippner reported a case study of a young child, already a fluent reader at an early age, who would have been declared unready to begin reading tuition had he been subjected to the then current reading readiness tests. There is probably no single aspect of most reading readiness tests that is an absolute barrier to learning to read for all children under all conditions. Many readiness tests have used perceptual tasks not involving the specific characteristics of print, thus distracting attention away from, rather than towards, the characteristics of written communication. Some tests of phonemic discrimination were based on judgement of similarity or difference in pairs of simple words or nonsense syllables. Additional factors come into play in more complex tests of auditory discrimination, where the child must make a comparison of a pair of words, and decide whether they are the same or different. In her study where the test involved judgement on pairs of phonemes, Hardy found a high overall performance even in young school beginners. An analysis of errors indicated that few phoneme pairs were contributing to the test difficulty (Hardy, 1973). She concluded that in some popular tests of auditory discrimination, factors other than auditory discrimination are being measured giving exaggerated estimates of auditory discrimination difficulties. In the present writer's study of young fluent readers, who could already read when they started school at five years of age, these children had no difficulty with a complex task of auditory discrimination (Clark, 1976).

Wilkinson (1971) considers that a systematic study of the relationship between reading and pre-reading oracy is important. Using a language involves knowing a great deal about what is likely to follow at any given point, knowledge of sequential probabilities on all levels of language. Greater understanding of the oral language development of children has resulted from an analysis of their errors and self-corrections in speech. In reading it is important that in children's early oral reading, their errors and self-corrections are monitored, and the types of errors under different initial approaches to learning to read are analysed. The work of Clay on the development of concepts of print in young children, and her research on the reconstruction of sentences by young school beginners when faced with tasks beyond their short-term memory are relevant to this aspect (see chapter 7 and Clay, 1972). More attention needs to be focused on whether this discrepancy is most marked when the initial reading materials give few linguistic cues.

The oral language of young children is, however, not the only relevant aspect when analysing readiness for reading. Consideration must also be given to the other aspects of language awareness, whether these can be systematically taught, and which approaches are most successful. Anticipation of the likely completion of a sentence or word is not dependent only on comprehension but operates also below that level in the area referred to as 'intermediate reading skills' (Merritt, 1970). Reading, for Smith (1971) involves predicting one's way through a passage of text, eliminating some alternatives in advance on the basis of knowledge of the redundancy in language, acquiring just enough visual information to eliminate the alternatives remaining. As in oral language, so also in reading, anticipation plays an important part. Indeed Goodman has referred to reading as a `psycholinguistic guessing game' (1970).

If one approaches the teaching of reading from an analysis of the skills and knowledge the child has already acquired when he begins learning to read, and of the additional knowledge and skills required for fluent reading, one may be led to the conclusion that some approaches to the teaching of reading miss crucial features required for the development of such a skill. Too much emphasis may be placed on training skills such as precise visual scanning of letters or words, while the important features may indeed be discrimination and anticipation rather than identification.

Children's progress in learning to read may well be influenced not only by the language of the reading materials, but also the language of reading instruction employed by the teacher. The studies of Reid (1960) and Downing (1969) showed limited grasp of the language of reading in the spoken language of pre-school children. A distinction must be made, however, between the language awareness required in order to learn the significant characteristics of print, and the language sophistication required to make sense of the sometimes complicated, and often imprecise, terminology in some early reading instruction. What is important is precise 'examples' and 'contrasts', as these apply in print, evidence, rather than instruction. The use of the words 'same' and 'different' may not be helpful to young learners (Smith 1971). For example, The, the and THE are different in some ways, but do not have the same significance in written language as the difference between d and b. Children usually learn to read in school and therefore in a group situation where certain features are common. Important variables may be over looked, others erroneously thought to be crucial. For this reason the present writer felt that a study of young children who could read on entry to school might shed light on aspects in the development of skilled reading that had not been appreciated (see chapters 4 and 5). The readiness of the child is only one aspect; the preparedness of the school to suit the instruction to the requirements of both task and child are worthy of more detailed investigation.

Language studies and teaching reading

Word counts of children's speech have on occasion been the basis for simplified content in children's early reading materials. Some reading schemes present frequent repetition of such words in simple sentence structures with progressive introduction of new words assumed to be already in the child's speaking vocabulary. Restriction of the initial reading experiences of a child to phonically regular words or word-like patterns enables a more systematic instruction in the structure and pattern of words to be developed. It provides the child with an independent, if limited, code-breaking strategy. Problems arise, however, in providing children with meaningful language in their reading material when only regular words are used, and in simple sentences. Many teachers use a combination of phonic and look-and-say approaches, differing in their emphasis and in the extent to which they base their phonics instruction on a systematic phonics programme or on incidental guidance as required (see chapters 15-18). Though research can provide lists of words from children's vocabularies for incorporation in initial reading schemes there are still problems.

Awareness of the difficulties of deprived and immigrant children led some teachers to develop their own reading materials based on the vocabulary of their particular children. A Schools Council Research Project led to the publication of *Breakthrough to Literacy*, based on language generated by the children (Mackay *et al*, 1970). Teachers using such approaches were referred to as `counsellors` by Southgate and Roberts in *Reading: which approach* (1970). Teachers classified by these authors as `instructors` are those using programmes and reading schemes for their teaching of beginning reading.

In some reading schemes the sentences are in reality only a structure into which to slot the necessary frequent repetitions of the basic sight vocabulary. Their limited sentence structure makes the stories less interesting than they might have been. Research has shown also that a range of sentence structures is used in the spoken language of pre-school children and a wide range of grammatical structures, even by so-called 'deprived' children. The 'un-English' structure of the stilted sentences in some reading schemes may lead to unpredictability. They may also prevent the child from developing appropriate strategies for detecting the sequential probabilities in written English. Studies of differential error patterns in children taught by a range of approaches could yield valuable information. (Clay, 1972)

Considerable emphasis has been placed by both teachers and parents on the value of reading aloud to young children as a preparation for early reading experiences. However, the focus was often on its motivational value, rather than of sensitizing children to features of written language through an oral medium. Reid (1972) drew attention to the possibility that reading aloud may have specific value in the pre-reading and early reading stages in familiarising the child with linguistic structures of written language presented orally. Such experience may well accelerate a child's reading progress in the early stages if appropriate reading materials arc then employed. Oral reading to older children with limited reading or language fluency may be important for their language development. Information, appreciation and relaxation are certainly three purposes in oral reading, but development of an intuitive awareness of written linguistic structures may also be important. Many parents stimulate their young children with a range of orally presented stories read to them; this is not so frequently continued when the children start school.

The concept of compensatory education

So often, attention has been centred on the deficiencies of the child in the learning situation and the inadequacies of the parents. To quote Bernstein (1970):

> The compensatory education concept serves to direct attention away from the internal organisation and the education context of the school, and focus our attention upon the families and children. Compensatory education implies that something is lacking in the family, and so in the child, and that as a result the children are

21

unable to benefit from schools (53-4). . . . We should stop thinking in terms of compensatory education but consider instead most seriously and systematically the conditions and contexts of the educational environment. (55)

It is important to appreciate that even language-deprived children from so-called inadequate homes have probably been bombarded with speech and that their deficiency is not, except in very rare instances, as a result of lack of experience of spoken language. In many such homes television provides an almost continuous pattern of speech. Pre-school children, even those whose language performance is limited, have in most instances acquired an appreciation of a wider range of linguistic structures than was previously appreciated. Thus two of the emphases in some programmes for deprived children, namely ample experiences of language, and models of grammatical structures for them to reproduce, are perhaps misplaced. The crucial features are to help the children to communicate using language with a range of recipients in a variety of situations. The children need to learn how to explain, and what questions to ask in order to receive further appropriate information. Studies on the effect of particular language situations on the quality and quantity of language produced by children are relevant here. The work of Donaldson and her co-workers in Edinburgh (Campbell and Wales, 1970) showed the effects on language production of specific situations. Kamii (1971) devised with pre-school children programmes for developing and testing their cognitive abilities that are less dependent on the limited language which the children may possess for expressing their solutions. Situation variables and their influence on spontaneity, length and complexity, style and content of language are discussed by Cazden under the heading, 'The neglected situation in child language, research and education' (in Williams, 1970). She considers the relevance of the topic, the task, and the listener to the quantity and complexity of language elicited. Clearly it is important that insights from research are utilized in developing language programmes within an educational context, whether oral or written. Blank (1970) also in *Language and Poverty*, claims that:

Thus, psycholinguists, like behaviourists provide an extremely limited empirical basis from which to derive guidelines for teaching language skills to children, whether disadvantaged or otherwise. The result has been that in the teaching of verbal abilities there has been an orientation similar to that in overall enrichment; namely, try to offer every possible language skill that may be important. (71)

She feels there are major problems in teaching higher-level cognition in a group setting except to children whose home has already provided and is providing a 'rich one-to-one verbal interchange'. In a group setting attention is diluted and sporadic and therefore will not provide the child with the essential stimulus and feed-back. Blank, like others, sees the learning difficulties of many children as:

reflecting the children's failure to develop a symbolic system which would permit them to see the plentiful stimulation already available to them, as existing in a coherent, logical and predictable framework. (73)

This is as significant in learning to read as it is in oral language development.

Features of successful teaching

Further investigation is required into the qualities and skills which characterise the successful language teacher so that as far as possible these skills can be developed by the training programmes in colleges. It is important to analyse the extent to which the teacher's own language is an important variable in the situation. Is there a 'deprived teacher' syndrome? Is this a significant factor in children's failures and could language enrichment programmes in colleges enrich and sensitize the teachers? What else is required of teachers to be successful in the type of role they are expected to fulfil? There is evidence from a variety of studies that the teaching of grammar even by a direct approach does not assist the development of children's written compositions. It is also possible that the teaching of linguistics to teachers in training may have disappointingly little effect on their teaching performance. Many student teachers may be no more ready or able to grasp the significance of linguistics than school children; as Morris wrote in 1973, 'You Can't Teach What You Don't Know'. The crucial question is, however, what must a teacher know? Research is needed into the extent to which, and the ways in which, teachers are influenced within their training by different content and forms of presentation.

We in education are too ready to accept the successes and ascribe the failures to the parents. Brandis and Henderson (1970) studied mothers' communications with their children at the preschool stage and then studied the children during their first three years in school. They found that social classes differed radically in their use of language for purposes of explanation and control and in the willingness of the mothers to respond to communications which their children initiated. Equally important, however, was the predictive value of an index of maternal communication *within* social class and for children of the same level of ability as measured by intelligence tests. There is need for more sophisticated and precise information on the extent to which maternal and paternal communication contributes to children's educational success. We have little opportunity of knowing how children from favoured home backgrounds would develop with regard to reading and related skills after the age of five without the intervention of formalised educational institutions.

Contributions of the home

For some members of the teaching profession the role of the parent is to prepare the child to be ready and willing to receive instruction; the concepts of readiness for school and reading readiness exemplify this outlook. In my research on fluent readers the embarrassment of a number of the parents at sending their child to school already reading fluently was distressing (Clark, 1976). Ready but not too ready seems to be the keynote. Once the child commences school, the role of the parent is seen by some professionals as providing 'interest', 'acceptance', and 'appreciation'. When evaluating the factors influencing success in reading we may be drawing erroneous conclusions if we concentrate only on the school environment. The contributions of the home to the learning situation should be measured in more sophisticated terms than numbers of visits to the school, number of books in the home, socioeconomic class, etc. Significant information might be obtained from studying the strategies in language tuition of successful parents—a little-tapped field of enquiry. Nursery education, it has been claimed makes children better able to benefit from primary education. There are dangers in any implication that parents do not or cannot provide language stimulation for their children; some do and others could.

Final comments

It is important that more sensitive and sophisticated measures be utilised in research projects into both oral language and reading progress, otherwise the weaknesses and the strengths of the children and of the teaching techniques will not be effectively analysed. There is need for more attention to the skills displayed by the fluent reader, together with an analysis of the extent to which any such reading is composed of distinguishable sub-skills. Particular attention should be paid to whether learning to read necessitates a sequential progression through a hierarchy of sub-skills to the final achievement of higher-order skills. It may be that some of these steps arc merely hurdles, or barriers, interspersed as a result of the types of approach employed in the teaching of reading. The present writer's study of children who learned to read fluently outside the school-group situation may throw some light on this question, as for example, most of them did not proceed from oral to silent reading. To quote Frank Smith:

> A clearer understanding of what the skilled reader can do, and of what the beginning reader is trying to do, is far more important for the reading teacher than any revision of instructional materials. (Smith, 1971: 230)

Selected points from the discussion (see Davies, 1975, 105-112)

Discussant, John E. Merritt: There are no fundamental points on which I would take issue with Clark except, perhaps, in matters of emphasis. Clark has pointed to certain deficiencies in tests of reading readiness and to the misleading nature of the information they provide. I would like to go further and question the value of the term 'reading readiness' itself. My reason for challenging the term is that it is so often taken to imply that readiness comes at some particular point of time.

Jessie Reid: May I make two branching points. One is the use of errors in helping us study the process of the acquisition of literacy as an intellectual feat. The other relates to what Bruner said in his paper about there being many different roads to a solution. Looking at errors is a very important way of trying to decide what different individuals are in fact doing. And this can be a contribution to the theoretical study of what it is to become literate.

Marie Clay: My own work and that of people like Goodman has produced evidence that may be running counter to the current stress on the value of semantics. This evidence indicates that the child in the very early stages of reading predicts the kind of word that will fit in with the structure more frequently, even when it is an error, than he predicts something which belongs to the same semantic field. Gradually, over the first few years of instruction, the errors tend to have the same visual form; many of the letters are the ones in the original text. They still have a syntactic equivalence but they are coming to have a very close semantic link too. Errors still occur but by now they indicate that children are looking for all three types of cue.

M. A. K. Halliday: I find that point very interesting. May I suggest that part of the reason for this finding may be the fact that a child has not yet at that early stage interpreted the reading operation as a linguistic one. In other words, he is not expecting it to produce meaning; and I think it is time to say that in a large amount of reading experience the child is decoding only at the structural level because he has not slotted it into his own language experience. ...I wonder if Clark would agree that we know very little about where reading experience fits into the child's functional experience with language? .... In functional terms I would say that reading comes to make sense as a necessary activity for the child when he sees how reading—and only reading—can open up new horizons for him. This is the only way, I think, in which reading readiness makes any sense.

James Britton: Whatever needs or functions arose that caused the human race to invent writing I think we need to look at a different set of functions that give the necessary motivation to children to learn to read. I think children learn to read because they want to read stories. A four-year-old son of a friend of mine was recently dictating a story to his mother, and one of the sentences was, 'The prince went sadly home, for he had nowhere else to go.' Obviously, 'for he had nowhere else to go,' was not something he had drawn from his speech; he had internalised written forms by listening to stories his mother read to him. He is already in the other language before going to school.

Margaret Clark: When I mentioned fluent readers I was not necessarily talking about gifted children, this is the interesting part of this study. These children came from all kinds of homes—what they have in common seems to be that their parents provide a very rich language environment. I agree with the comment that too much stress has been placed on oral reading. We need it in order to specify errors but we do not need to make children learn to read orally. I have asked the mothers of these fluent readers, 'When did you know he could read?' Several have replied, `I didn't realise for a while, and then he asked me what that word was. I wondered why he asked about that one and then I realised he knew all the others`.

References

Bernstein, B. (1970) `A sociolinguistic approach to socialisation: with some reference to educability`. In F. Williams (ed) *Language and Poverty: perspectives on a theme.* Chicago: Markham Publishing: 25-61.

Blank, M. (1970) `Some philosophical influences underlying preschool intervention for disadvantaged children`. In F. Williams (ed) *Language and Poverty: perspectives on a theme.* Chicago: Markham Publishing: 62-80.

Brandis, W. and Henderson, D. (1970) *Social Class, Language and Communication.* London: Kegan Paul.

Campbell, R. and Wales, R. (1970) `The study of language acquisition`. In J. Lyons (ed) *New Horizons in Linguistics.* Harmondsworth: Penguin.

Cazden, C. B. (1970) `The neglected situation in child language research and education`. In F. Williams (ed) *Language and Poverty: perspectives on a theme.* Chicago: Markham Publishing: 81-101.

Clark, M. M. (1976) *Young Fluent Readers: what can they teach us?* London: Heinemann Educational. NB This research was referred to during the seminar. A publisher who had been present, offered to publish this book.

Clay, M. M. (1972) *Reading: the patterning of complex behaviour.* Auckland: Heinemann Educational.

Downing, J. (1969) `How children think about reading`, *The Reading Teacher,* 23 (iii): 217-230.

Downing, J. and Thackray, D. V. (1971) *Reading Readiness.* London: University of London Press.

Goodman, K. S. (1970) `Reading: a psycholinguistic guessing game`. In H. Singer and R. B. Ruddell (eds) *Theoretical Models and Processes of Reading.* Newark, Delaware: International Reading Association.

Hardy, M.I. (1973) `The development of beginning reading skills: recent findings`. In M. M. Clark and A. Milne (eds) *Reading and Related Skills.* London. Ward Lock Educational: 46-56.

Kamii, C K. (1971) `Evaluation of learning in pre-school education: socio-emotional, perceptual-motor, cognitive development`. In B. S. Bloom, J. T. Hastings and G.F. Madaus (eds) *Handbook on Formative and Summative Evaluation of Student Learning.* New York: McGraw-Hill: 283-344.

Krippner, S. (1963) `The boy who read at eighteen months`. *Exceptional Children.* November: 105-109.

Mackay, D. Thompson, B. and Schaub, P. (1970) *Breakthrough to Literacy.* London: Longman.

Merritt, J. E. (1970) `The intermediate skills`. In K. Gardner (ed) *Reading Skills: theory and practice.* London: Ward Lock Educational: 42-63.

Morris, J. M. (1973) `You can`t teach what you don`t know. In M. M. Clark and A. Milne (eds) *Reading and Related Skills.* London: Ward Lock Educational: 105-112.

Reid, J. F. (1960) `Learning to think about reading`, *Educational Research,* 9: 56-62.

Reid, J. F. (1972) `Children`s comprehension of syntactic features found in some extension readers`. In J.F. Reid (ed) *Reading Problems and Practices.* London: Ward Lock Educational: 394-403.

Smith, F. (1971) *Understanding Reading: a psycholinguistic analysis of reading and learning to read.* New York: Holt, Rinehart and Winston.

Southgate, V. and Roberts, J. R. (1970) *Reading: which approach?* London: University of London Press.

Wilkinson, A. (1971) *The Foundations of Language.* London: Oxford University Press.

Chapter 4

Strengths and Weaknesses of Children with Reading Difficulties and Young Fluent Readers

This is an edited version of a paper in *Reading, Writing and Multiculturalism,* 1982, D. Burns, A. Campbell and R. Jones, (eds). Adelaide: Australian Reading Association.

Background to educational research

Educational research reports are frequently criticised either as being couched in technical terms (or jargon), as being too complex (or simplistic), as being irrelevant, or failing to confirm 'facts' clearly supported by common sense. In order to assess the value of any educational research it is important to have adequate information on the research questions posed, the sample, methods and results and the validity of the conclusions on the basis of that particular study. Only when the scientific respectability of the study has been established is the generalizability to other countries, ages or types of children a matter for consideration. Finally it is important to distinguish statistical significance of results from their educational significance and to realise that it is possible in research with large enough samples to obtain statistically significant results where the difference in performance between groups is very small, or to have large differences between groups in average scores but to have considerable overlap in performance between the groups.

The dangers of over-generalisation of educational research are as serious as ignoring its evidence. Perhaps an example will clarify this point. It may be possible to establish in a study, and repeat with similar results, that a particular new reading method involving considerable expenditure of money may raise the reading level of seven-year-old children by a statistically significant amount. If the actual difference were to be a month or so in reading accuracy then surely the educational significance of the results should still be open to question? All too often this aspect of research is not considered; indeed frequently the aspects of research that obtain publicity

31

are those that fit in with politically expedient decisions, sometimes ones that have already been made.

Another danger in drawing implications from educational research, that is explored here, is that of assuming features that are found in children who fail are necessarily explanations for their failure, or that they would inevitably be a cause of failure. Screening, readiness tests and predictions from achievement tests are so often framed within this pattern of expectation. It seems important to consider not only the weaknesses of the children who fail but both the strengths and the weaknesses of those who succeed. These issues are explored here with illustrations from my two researches *Reading Difficulties in Schools* (Clark, 1970 new edition, 1979) and *Young Fluent Readers* (Clark, 1976). Both these publications are the actual research reports, therefore open to scrutiny for their scientific rigour and generalizability.

Background to the two researches

The focus here is on insights from a comparison of two studies, one of children who failed to learn to read, the other of children who entered school already reading silently and with understanding. A brief discussion of these two studies will set the context for consideration of more recent developments in my own and related researches. The focus will be on increasing awareness of the features of the child, the parents, teachers and the learning situation which together determine not only whether a child can read and write, but whether this is a meaningful and enjoyable experience.

Anyone who appreciates the important distinctions between spoken and written language will not be surprised to find the style of this paper very different from the spoken presentation. This distinction made between the spoken and written versions has a wider significance than merely a justification that the two versions are not identical. Perhaps one of the dangers of the suggestion frequently made that print is just 'speech written down' is that this does not do justice to either as a form of communication in its own right. The purely visual features of print have perhaps been overstressed, while the importance of acquiring sensitivity to prediction within written language in learning to read is not fully recognised. The rather stilted 'speech written down' type of products seen in the work of some older children who were late in learning to read and did not have a compensatory experience of written language read aloud may be partly the result of this lack of sensitivity. The quality of written language produced by the early reader with a wide experience of the language of books may owe more than we have recognised to extensive and rewarding experience of written language.

One important compensatory aspect in the education of the low progress child could be an enriched experience of print through the spoken medium. In this way experience of print could be achieved at an earlier age and enriched educational experiences made available. In the twenty-first century we now have through the medium of computers greater possibilities than were available in 1980s. All too often children who are slow to learn to read have a diet confined to their failures, thus confirming assumptions by those around them of their limited potential.

Reading difficulties in schools

The study

It is important to set the first of the two research studies in its historical context. It was undertaken in the mid-1960s at a time when there was controversy concerning 'dyslexia' or the extent of severe and prolonged reading difficulty in children of average intelligence. There was a tendency to conceive of this within a medical 'disease' model with assumptions of specific symptoms common to such children in what was claimed to be a widespread disorder, and it was suggested that one or a few specific methods should prove effective. Most studies at that time had been clinic studies of highly selected cases, studies in which there was no information on the characteristics of the population from which these children came. If diagnosed by a medical practitioner as having reading difficulty a child was likely to be labelled dyslexic; the same child if diagnosed by a psychologist was likely to be referred to as a backward reader. For this reason a community study of a large population with children studied individually, over time seemed important. The starting point was identification of all children within a complete population in a given area who after two years at school had still failed to acquire independent reading skill.

The study initially involved 1,544 children aged seven years of age, all of whom had started school at the same time. Up-to-date incidence figures were collected for a number of features claimed to have an association with delayed reading. All the children in this research were tested individually and the study involved over eighty people assisting either in the testing or analysis. A number of those who helped in the initial testing were students. Because of the nature of the research questions, the children who were studied further until nine years of age were those who in spite of average intelligence continued to have difficulty in reading. Among the findings of this study were the following:

- there were few such children in that population;
- their difficulties were widespread rather than confined to the reading situation;
- the pattern of difficulties was not consistent across the group;
- there was little evidence of active parental involvement;
- the majority were boys (14 boys and 5 girls).

What can we learn from this study?

This study provided answers to a number of the questions posed and because of the way it was designed it was possible to generalise some of the results. Such a study does not, however, make it possible to establish whether there was any causal link between the difficulties those children showed when tested already failing and their reading progress. It was not possible to determine to what extent their widespread difficulties either caused, or were caused by their reading failure. It is so easy to assume that if a range of difficulties and deficiencies, whether in the child or the home, are frequently seen in children who fail that the two are causally linked. Furthermore each time one subsequently sees a failing child these are the very features that one tends to notice.

Long-term studies commencing before the children fail, or succeed are needed to explore this. So many studies have included only the failures and possibly a control group of average children. There may be features in the school situation where most children learn to read, whether it be the group situation, the age at which that are expected to learn to read, or the method used, that make certain weaknesses or strengths seem crucial. For these reasons I felt it was important to study a group of children who had learnt to read before coming to school, not only at an earlier age but not in a group learning situation.

Young fluent readers

The study

In this second research, a small group of children who were reading fluently with understanding before starting school was studied intensively. The aim was not only to consider their strengths but also weaknesses in spite of which they had learnt to read. It would be as dangerous to over-simplify the findings of this second study of 32 early readers as to minimise the complexity of the causes of failing readers. It is worth highlighting the following characteristics before turning to implications of the two studies:

- their abilities were wide, not confined to reading;
- while few had been instructed in reading, parental support and involvement was evident;
- their strengths appeared to be in oral language rather than visuo-motor, and particularly a sensitivity to sequential patterns in language; the majority here were also boys.

To highlight the significance of a study such as this in the climate in which it was undertaken, it is worth quoting just one example, namely a boy from a supportive but, by some categorisations, 'limited' home, a difficult birth, concussion at three years of age, and not least doubtful handedness. Yet at under five years of age, before starting school, this child could read on the level of an eleven year old! All these are characteristics to which, had he been a failure, at that time, the failure might have been attributed. It is important to be cautious in predicting failure and to avoid using screening tests that could be failed by a child who is already reading fluently. The rich and varied information gained from a study of children such as these young fluent readers needs a more detailed analysis than is possible here. However, a few insights will be given. (See also chapter 5).

The parents of these children found it difficult to identify exactly when their children could read or how they had learnt. When the children were asked what they did if they did not know a word, answers such as 'guess', 'miss it out', 'ask someone' were offered, all of which highlight ways of utilising the redundancy of written language if the motivation to explore it is present. Indeed for the last word in a sentence, frequently at most discrimination of the first letter is all that is required for the word to be identified. This raises issues not only about strategies that it may be valuable to encourage, but about the type of reading material that it might be valuable to encourage young children to explore in the early stages of learning to read. The differences between `scheme readers`, and even relatively simple `real books`, are important. The complexity of the text in a book, may aid understanding rather than necessarily making it more difficult for a child to understand. This is important also for the older reader of limited reading ability. An apparently simplified text may not only make the material less stimulating but also, more difficult. This point is discussed in a paper by Gardner (in Clark and Glynn, 1980). The fact that the young fluent readers did not use instructional texts is not an argument that they may be without benefit for any children. What is being stressed, however, is that complexity of language does not necessarily make for greater difficulty, nor simplified text for ease.

The evidence that the young fluent readers appeared to read silently even in the early stages should also serve as a challenge as to the function of reading aloud by children. Can we any longer assume that the natural progression is from reading aloud to reading softly then only later, silently? Oral reading by the child may give sensitive teachers insights into children`s development of self-correction strategies, provided they listen to the children and encourage them to predict, using all the cues at their disposal.

Perhaps we may have over-emphasised the importance of reading aloud by the child as an essential part of the process of learning to read. However, reading aloud to the child may be an important aspect of reading instruction rather than a frill to be omitted if time is short.

The developing competence in spelling of these young fluent readers also has lessons for us. They were beginning to show a competence in spelling, also an ability to attempt words using a plausible substitute spelling, how the word might have been spelt in English. Equally important they knew what they did not know. Again, the fact that spelling was being caught by these children does not mean that other children may not need to be taught to spell. Spelling is an eminently teachable subject approached through the route of plausible alternatives in the language being studied. So many poor spellers do not even know when they are right! It would be misleading to confuse the mechanics of writing with the ability to write creatively, or to communicate explicitly in the written medium. A person does need at least a minimum competence in spelling in order to be understood and freed to be creative. Evidence of a developing competence in written language was found in these young fluent readers as they were followed through their first years at school.

The samples of written work by these children at seven or eight years of age provided by the school showed graphically the effects of their reading. Clearly the extent to which this found expression in school and was developed further owed a great deal to the sensitivity of the teachers, the situations they created for writing and the tasks they set. At an earlier stage many of these children could already simulate in dictating into a tape-recorder, the style of their favourite authors' written language. It is important to draw attention also to one of the children who while talking in this setting used his colloquial language, and what to some would have been regarded as bad grammar. Yet he was able to capture the flavour of Tom Sawyer which he had enjoyed reading. This same child when writing was quite capable of using complex sentences and an appropriate range of vocabulary.

What can we learn from these children?

Let us not assume that the only route to competence in written language is via fluency in spoken language. A possible route to literacy may be initially through experience of written language presented orally, while avoiding interfering with the child's spoken language initially. Wide experience of listening to book language may have considerable potential for such children. One valuable feature of the language of books is its invariant nature as compared with subtle but misleading changes on repetition of a message in spoken language. This approach using orally presented written language would not threaten the child's culture. At a later stage the child is more likely himself to become aware of the appropriateness of different registers for different situations.

Oral language competence as an essential step towards reading may be questioned; perhaps its place in the development of writing competence has been over-stressed. The difficulty for the older child who has previously been a poor reader in producing written language may owe something to lack of sensitivity to the particular features of written language. It may also, however, owe something to the contexts in which we expect children in school to produce written language. Few are allowed the opportunity to draft and re-draft as part of the creation of written language; even if allowed it may only have a proof reading role of improving approximation to an already envisaged correct model. Had I submitted to a publisher my first, or even my fourth draft of *Young Fluent Readers*, it would certainly not have been accepted! The development of ideas in written form is of value not only as a communication but also as an aid to the development of thought.

Last but certainly not least in discussion of what we can learn from a study of these young fluent readers, is the contribution of their parents and other adults around them. The contribution was not necessarily in material things, and certainly not always in a plentiful supply of books bought for the child. The interaction between the children and these adults was impressive, and print was clearly seen as a part, and indeed an important aspect of the environment. One challenge in school is that we as teachers create as much as possible of the stimulating, non-threatening atmosphere of the good home.

Lessons from educational research

It has been possible to develop only a few selected themes from these researches. Finally I would like to consider briefly what we can learn from educational research, from children, from teachers and not least from parents. The model in educational research was for many years one of measurement and prediction; of ability and attainment. Bloom (1979), argued for `New Directions in Educational Research`, stressing the importance of considering alterable variables. No longer can one assume the constancy of the IQ in face of the studies in which it has been used as a measure of the effectiveness of pre-school intervention studies. Caution is needed in drawing implications about individuals from group tests. These may have value in observing group trends, but in the light of growing knowledge of the influence of the situation, the task and the listener on language, caution is needed in their interpretation. Deductions about differences between groups, for example middle class and working class, or boys and girls, based on overall scores are dangerous.

It is important to explore explanations for the child who is outstanding in a group where this was not predicted. Bloom's conception of research is dynamic rather than static. This argues for more studies of individual children such as *Cushla and her Books* (Butler 1979) in which with sensitivity, the environment and development of a pre-school handicapped child is explored, or *GNYS AT WRK* (Bissex, 1980) in which Bissex studied the development of her son Paul`s writing prior to starting school. In their study *Inside the Primary Classroom,* Galton, Simon and Croll (1980), interaction between different teachers and different children is explored dynamically. Donachy, in a pioneering study on the potential of parents previously regarded as inadequate to play an important role in their preschool children`s development, showed this could have a significant effect both on their own self-image and the attitude of the teachers to those parents with whom they had become involved. This is reported in Clark and Cheyne (1979).

The limited reference to the teacher in this chapter should not be taken to mean a devaluation of the role of the teacher, on the contrary, the aim was to stress the importance of the learning situations in which children find themselves within both the home and in school. Just as it is argued that the high progress child is a child who self-corrects (Clay 1969), so the good teacher is not one who never makes mistakes, we all do that, but one who learns from their mistakes and as Hunter describes it in *Reading and Writing for the Child with Difficulties* (in Clark and Glynn eds. 1980) learns to read not only books but to read children.

The mood of this paper is one of optimism and one in which education is seen as a dynamic process where there are no right answers or static solutions. The skill of the teacher is to capitalise on and to develop the strengths of individual children, aware of and sensitive to the contribution of the parents to the process of education. Marie Clay refers to reading as 'A Patterning of Complex Behaviour', (Clay 1979); so also is teaching.

References

Bissex, G. L. (1980) *GNYS AT WRK: a child learns to read and write.* Cambridge, Mass: Harvard University Press.

Bloom, B. S. (1979) *Alterable Variables: the new direction in educational research.* Edinburgh: The Scottish Council for Research in Education.

Butler, D. (1979) *Cushla and her Books.* Auckland: Hodder and Stoughton.

Clark, M. M. (1970) *Reading Difficulties in Schools.* Penguin. Second Edition, London: Heinemann Educational, 1979.

Clark, M. M. (1976) *Young Fluent Readers: what can they teach us?* London: Heinemann Educational.

Clay, M. M. (1969) `Reading errors and self-correction behaviour`, *British Journal of Educational Psychology*, Vol 39: 47-56.

Clay, M. M. (1972) *Reading: the Patterning of Complex Behaviour.* Auckland: Heinemann Educational Books. (second edition 1979).

Donachy, W. (1979) `Parental participation in pre-school education`. In M. M. Clark and W. M. Cheyne (eds) *Studies in Pre-school Education.* London: Hodder and Stoughton: 122-149.

Galton, M., Simon, B., Croll, P. (1980) *Inside the Primary Classroom.* London: Routledge and Kegan Paul.

Gardner, K. (1980) `Failure to read: not reading failure`. In M. M. Clark and T. Glynn (eds) *Reading and Writing for the Child with Difficulties.* University of Birmingham: Educational Review Occasional Publications, No.8. Birmingham: University of Birmingham: 11-15.

Hunter, C. M. (1980) `Becoming a better teacher of children with learning difficulties`. In M. M. Clark and T. Glynn (eds) *Reading and Writing for the Child with Difficulties.* University of Birmingham: Educational Review Occasional Publications No.8: 55-66.

Chapter 5
Insights from Young Fluent Readers

This chapter is based on a chapter in *Awakening to Literacy*, 1984, H. Goelman, A. Oberg and F. Smith (eds): 122-130. Victoria, British Columbia: The University of Victoria.

Background

This chapter extends the discussion in the previous chapter where I compared the strengths and weaknesses of children with reading difficulties and young children who were already reading with fluency and understanding when they started school at five years of age. Here the focus is on additional insights from the study of the young fluent readers, based on further analysis from the research for a symposium in Canada, some not reported in *Young Fluent Readers* (Clark, 1976). A growing interest in the development of writing in young preschool children became apparent in authors who had previously published on reading (Smith, 1983) and also increased interest in a possible reciprocal relationship between reading and writing (Clay, 1980; Bissex, 1980). By 1970, the process of learning to read rather than the best method of teaching reading became the focus of much research; likewise a growing awareness of the insights that may be gained, by studying in depth the development of children who make rapid progress toward literacy, including children who already read with fluency, understanding, and interest on entry to school. My study was an in-depth study of a small group of children (twenty boys and twelve girls), all of whom were already reading fluently and with understanding on entry to school at approximately 5 years of age (Clark, 1976). Many of these children showed limited motor coordination and therefore could write or print only with limited success from an aesthetic point of view, but most were showing evidence of a growing awareness of the sequential probabilities of letter arrangements in English words. Already at between 5 and 6 years of age and before formal instruction in spelling, most of these children could spell a number of simple words correctly, and provide plausible alternatives to correct spellings within the conventions of English spelling, as evidenced by their errors. They showed awareness of what they did not know and, in some cases, an unwillingness to attempt a word they were sure they did not know.

The parents of these children were interviewed as the children started school and again approximately two years later. Information also was obtained on the children's school progress for another two years, providing valuable insights into the relationship of their early reading and wide range of reading to their development of competence in written language. It was tempting to continue the study for a longer period, but it became apparent that there was a danger of adversely affecting at least some of these children and their families by such intense observation. However, I decided that a further study of some of the evidence gathered in that study, particularly the reports of the parental interviews and the children's attempts at spelling, would be valuable.

Some of the observations in this chapter are based on just such a reappraisal. One publication that led to my decision was the study by Bissex (1980) of her own son's early attempts at spelling, particularly her reports of the lack of vowels in his earliest attempts to communicate in writing, his use of uppercase rather than lowercase letters, and his early inventive spelling before he began to appreciate that there is a correct way to spell a word.

The young fluent readers and their parents

As might have been expected, some of the children in my study who read fluently were from professional homes and an environment providing an extensive and varied range of books. Some had older brothers or sisters who already were experiencing success in school. There was, however, great variety in the children's backgrounds, the size of their families, and their position within the families. One striking feature about all the parents interviewed was their interest in their families and how interesting they themselves were as they discussed, with knowledge .and sensitivity, their children's experiences. In some homes, siblings had learned to read early, were succeeding in school, and were available as models and even potential teachers of their young brothers or sisters. Some parents contrasted the early reader with his or her siblings in terms of memory and powers of intense concentration.

Many sources and types of print were cited by the parents as arousing their child's interest. In most homes, the local library was included among the sources of printed material. Most parents used the library themselves and introduced their children to it. For the most part, children chose their own books with encouragement from their parents. Parents reported that these children had many interests, including playing with other children, unless they were too absorbed in something else! A review of the parents' answers to the questions in the structured interview revealed the parents' pleasure in their families and that they could express that pleasure with quality language, regardless of their social class and however limited their schooling. One mother of five young children commented during the interview: `Who would do housework when you could play with children?` Another commented: `I was a latchkey child; I'd never do that to my children`. In the parents' comments, the children's memory and power of observation were stressed, as was their ability and desire to concentrate. A father commented, `He always surprises me`, and a mother said, `I think it's an enquiring mind that's did it.` (that is, caused him to learn to read at an early age).

Most parents had observed significant incidents and could retell them graphically, revealing the quality of the interactions in the family. Their sensitivity was apparent in the specifics of their children's learning which they could recount. One child interested in the Bible was reported to note the use of the word spake rather than spoke. Another, at a later stage, was interested to know the meaning of a Latin phrase in a novel about school days. From the context, it was clear that in incidents such as these, a dialogue had taken place with extended learning, as far as the child could and wished to develop it.

Shared enjoyment was reported by a mother who had left school at an early age but later studied English literature in the evenings. She described with pleasure how her life was enriched by books and how, when her son was about 7 years old, they could sit together for up to one and a half hours reading and not speaking. Television (even the much-maligned advertisements) was clearly a stimulus to many children. One parent commented, `It's amazing what he culls from that` (referring to television advertisements). One parent described her child's `love of learning`, and another described his child's breadth of knowledge and early development of literacy as `kind of scarey`. Yet another parent described the child's great memory for things that happened, `for seeing and hearing,` whereas another said, `He corrected us, not we correcting him; he has a marvellous memory.` The shared experiences in which all these comments are embedded are particularly impressive.

The children and their reading

The quality of the children's comprehension of print is perhaps best illustrated by the following examples: One child was reported to have read a poster in a bus which stated, `Friday night is danger night`. His response had been, `It's a good job it's Saturday`. The second child, younger than 5 years, was reported by his teacher to have read silently a letter for his mother that she handed to him. In the letter, the teacher mentioned the 7-year period over which they would have contact. The boy had remarked in a tone of utmost concern, `Whew! Seven whole years!`

Although the children had high scores for both accuracy and comprehension in the conventional reading tests, such tests failed to capture the quality of their literacy. Isolated passages to be read orally in a formal setting cannot recreate the quality of these children's response to print. I question the use of such artificial text as that in standard reading tests and the value of assessment by oral reading tests as a measure of the reading competence of these children. Some of these children normally read silently for meaning. Indeed, some had developed reading competence without resorting to any prolonged period of oral reading that the parents could recall. Studies of these young children's responses to elaborate story structure and of their growing awareness of how to predict the ideas and even precise words and sentences in written language, made me even more uneasy at artificially created print as a medium for early reading instruction. The range of `real-world print` from which these children learned and to which they responded was impressive. To ensure that print becomes a dynamic and significant part of the school environment is an important challenge if most children are to become literate and want to read both for information and enjoyment.

The children and their spelling

Unfortunately it did not occur to me to ask the parents for samples of the children's written communications from preschool. Thus, all I had of the children's writing was the conventional spelling test set as part of the research shortly after they entered school. Most parents reported that their children had some interest in writing, primarily as an extension rather than a precursor of reading. Pens, pencils, crayons, and blackboards had been of interest to most, as had word games. Some parents commented that their children wrote in uppercase letters although they read lowercase letters. One parent whose child used a mixture made the observation, `You need to be very artful to read it`. Most parents suggested that lowercase letters were beginning to be used only since the child's entry to school. In my book I did make reference to the children's spelling on the conventional test, and that most children could spell many of the words. They also tended to be sensitive to what they could not spell, and most errors bore some resemblance to the intended word. Prior to the seminar in Canada I made a further study of the attempts at spelling of these thirty-two children in the light of research I had read about the early development of spelling, particularly Bissex's (1980) description of her own son's early spelling attempts.

Within this group of thirty-two children, there were some who used uppercase letters consistently for each word written, and some, (relatively few), who used lowercase letters for all words. In addition, there were children who used a capital letter at the beginning of some words or all capital letters for some words. A sizeable number of words, even those spelled correctly, had a mix of uppercase and lowercase letters (for example, BeG, friEnd, womeN, lOuD). This variation was apparent even in children with a spelling age of more than nine years. One child wrote, ARE, SEEM, FOR, but Chop, Ship, and who. Another wrote ANy and GReAT. Given the fairly poor coordination of a number of these children, it was difficult to determine whether some letters were indeed uppercase where only the size distinguishes the two forms.

These atypical uses of letter case probably should not be considered errors at this stage of the children's literacy development. Rather, it is more appropriate to consider what they illustrate of these children's awareness of the critical features in letter discrimination. Their spelling attempts show clearly their awareness that e and E are similar, in terms of reading, in ways that A is not, and that D and d share critical features for reading that b and d do not. Most of the children had developed sufficient awareness of spelling patterns to attempt successfully words such as beg and even ship and food as well as common irregular words such as the and are. However, words such as who gave difficulties to a number: It was spelled Ho, HWO, Hoo, or HOW. When incorrect, the spelling of date often was DAT, and a common incorrect rendering of done was DUN. Any was sometimes ENY or EANY. Even a word such as women was spelled correctly by eleven of the thirty-two children, whereas eight would not attempt it, possibly knowing their own limitations, and the remainder wrote it as WOMAN, WOMIN, WIMN, wumen (a very Scottish rendering), or WIMEN; only one gave Wmn (without a vowel).

In view of the comments by Bissex (1980) in *GNYS AT WRK* it was interesting to observe that these young children were at the stage of being able to spell regular words and common irregular words and that they used vowels as well as consonants in most spelling attempts, often using a vowel which, if wrong, might still have been possible. By their earliest school years, they had an appreciation of critical features of words. The superficial appearance of their attempts at spelling, including large writing, a mixture of uppercase and lowercase letters of varying size, and some variation in alignment, could easily mask the children's increasing mastery of the written features of English. Furthermore, in a situation such as this in which their attention was only on spelling, the children were more likely to show the

48

extent of their potential and grasp of the conventions of English spelling. The quality of their attempts to generate communication in writing might well have been equally impressive in a different context. However, in such creative situations, it is not likely they would have succeeded in sustaining the same level of competence in the surface features such as spelling where there attention was on content. Thus, as described by one parent, `you would have to be artful to read it`.

One dilemma faced by schools receiving children as advanced as these is how to help the children retain sensitivity to their errors and improve their command over the surface features without destroying their wish to communicate in writing for a variety of purposes. The issue is no less important with children whose literacy is less developed on entry to school but who also may have developed a form of written communication for purposes important to them, even if the spelling is less conventional and the communication less meaningful to others. Bissex (1980) and Smith (1982) examined the competing claims of these two necessary aspects of written communication.

Extending literacy at school

All the children in the young fluent reader study (Clark, 1976) entered school with two things in common: the ability and the desire to read at a very early age. In few other ways were they similar. From discussions with teachers, parents, and the children themselves, it was clear that the school as a learning environment presented difficulties for some of these children. There were those who found it unchallenging or boring, and others who chose not to display too much of their undoubted talent to avoid appearing very different from their classmates. Some consideration of the needs, abilities, and features in the environment of exceptional children such as these may provide insights towards developing a stimulating environment in school for all children. In this way many more children could learn to read, learn from reading, and enjoy the wide range of shared experiences that could be opened up for them by literacy.

Literacy for these young fluent readers involved a wide range of materials and was used to develop a wide range of interests. As one father reported, `brain books` fascinated one child, and telephone directories, another. Newspapers were a source of information to several children, for events in the outside world and, more immediately, for the times of their favourite television programmes. This latter source was likely to be of continuing interest only as long as there was an element of real choice that the youngsters could exercise, with the hope of actually viewing programmes of their choice. One child was interested in predicting sports results which he then checked. Some read to themselves stories they had enjoyed previously, and others read stories that would not have been read to them yet. Thus the children's reading was an enjoyable part of their environment for varied purposes, and it was an activity that extended opportunities for learning facts and information they considered relevant to themselves.

On entering school, most children already belonged to the local library, as did other family members. Their views on the books they wished to read were regarded as important. As one father put it when asked about his child's choice, `He is fussy too`. Access to the library, advice, and encouragement were all there, but choice to a great extent belonged to the children and was related to and varied with their other interests.

Implications for other children

The quality of environment and interaction with adults that these study children experienced also was available, in most instances, to their brothers and sisters. Although many of the siblings did not read before entering school, many did so shortly after, and they seemed to make good progress in school. Some would be regarded as successes of the school, of course, but it is clear just how much their readiness and receptiveness had developed from the breadth of experiences in the home. This was highlighted when, after the completion of the research, I had occasion to visit the home of one family in which there were four children, the boy in the study being the youngest. I noted there was no bookcase full of books in the small living room, but there were a number of books borrowed from the local library by all six members of the family who clearly enjoyed reading and shared their reading experiences with one another. The progress in literacy development by the youngest boy's siblings had been impressive, and although they had learned to read within school, it is important not to underestimate the contribution of their stimulating home environment. On talking to the father, whom I had not met previously, I realized that I had failed to appreciate his contribution to this environment. He had left school early and had an unskilled job. Nonetheless, he was fascinated by books and confessed that he had read fairy stories to the children partly because it gave him an excuse to read them as he enjoyed them. Like the others I had met, he described in amusing terms how his young son had used his early reading skills, in this instance, to help an elderly neighbour to place her bets!

Had it been possible to study over a period of years two children from each of these homes, the child who could read on entering school and another who could not, further valuable insights could have been gained regarding how to stimulate literacy and how to bridge home experience to school experience in the development of literacy.

Language growth before school

It should be remembered that my study of young fluent readers was retrospective. Studies of preschool children such as that of her daughter by Payton (1984) show in some young pre-school children a growing awareness of the potential in their written communication. Some of Cecilia`s written messages were understood only by the child herself, acting as a temporary reminder, and were soon forgotten; there were examples of interrelated drawing and writing, each serving a specific purpose. At the age of 3 years 2 months, a letter given to the child's mother seemed a genuine milestone, a confirmation of Cecilia's appreciation that writing serves a real-world purpose. Writing's value as a form of communication was further evidenced in Cecilia's desire to prepare a shopping list and particularly in her response to her mother's query as to whether she would write sweets: `It doesn't matter. We won't forget sweets`, she said. There are lessons in this example for teachers who may not always ensure that the writing they require of young children has a real purpose as a communication with others or, alternatively, a function as a reminder to the child. At this pre-school stage, even before she could read, it was apparent that Cecilia was aware of the differences in these forms of communication. Her awareness of her growing competence was evidenced in her announcement one day at teatime: `I can cut my egg now 'cause I can write my name`.

Final comment

It is a challenge for schools to provide stimulating environments that are responsive to the search for meaning for all the children, particularly those less fortunate than those discussed here. Teachers in their promotion of literacy in an inevitably more formal environment than the home, and with competing claims of the various children at different levels of language development, need to plan creative contexts within which the children can develop and extend their literary skills. There are insights to be gleaned from those children who learn to read before entry to school. See chapters 8 and 10 for practical examples, based on research, of ways to create a stimulating environment in school for young children learning to read.

References

Bissex, G. L. (1980) *GNYS AT WRK: a child learns to read and write.* Cambridge, Mass: Harvard University Press.

Clark, M. M. (1970) *Reading Difficulties in Schools.* London: Heinemann Educational.

Clark, M. M. (1976) *Young Fluent Readers: what can they teach us?* London: Heinemann Educational.

Clay, M. M. (1980) `Early writing, and reading: reciprocal gains`. In M. M. Clark and T. Glynn (eds) *Reading and Writing for the Child with Difficulties.* Educational Review, Occasional Publications 8. Birmingham: University of Birmingham.

Payton, S. (1984) *Developing Awareness of Print: a young child`s first steps towards literacy*. Educational Review Off set publication 2. Birmingham: University of Birmingham.

Smith, F. (1982) *Writing and the Writer*. London: Heinemann.

Section II
Young Literacy Learners: how we can help them

There are five chapters in this section, the first two of which set the background for the remaining three chapters, and include research references. Few references are cited in chapters 8 and 10; however, the ideas discussed there are based on researches referred to in Section I. Chapters 8 and 10 feature practical work either I or my students carried out in primary schools and with pre-school children. My aim is to show there can be a direct link between insights from research and practice.

Chapter 6, `Literacy learning in creative contexts`, is based on a paper I gave in Lund in 1987, later published in *Children's Creative Communication,* R. Söderbergh (ed). 1988.

Chapter 7, `Sensitive observation and the development of literacy`, is a tribute to Marie Clay, whose plea for sensitive observations of children from their earliest encounters with literacy, and her early intervention programme, Reading Recovery, attracted interest in many parts of the world beyond New Zealand where they were first developed. That chapter is based on two articles published in *Literacy Today* in 2007. They are published here with permission from Education Publishing.

In the *Education Journal* March 2014 Issue 192: 14, there is a brief report of a new study of long term effectiveness of a Reading Recovery programme in New Zealand. Early intervention was not on its own sufficient. It is claimed that progress is maintained where, `it is part of a planned and coherent school-wide literacy strategy in which students are meticulously monitored and provided with targeted support over the years following an intensive intervention`. This has relevance beyond Reading Recovery, and would apply to the current policy in England. (see Section IV).

In chapter 8, `Meeting individual needs in learning to read`, a number of aspects of importance for children learning to read are discussed with suggestions for practical work with children from pre-school to primary. A few illustrations of writing and drawing by young children are included. The ideas in that chapter were reported in my book *Young Literacy Learners: how we can help them,* published in 1994. This followed a period when I worked as a volunteer in an inner city school; there I endeavoured to stimulate a class of seven and eight-year-old children's interest in literacy without the use of any expensive materials. Some of the illustrations in that book, and here came from teachers with whom I worked.

In chapter 9, 'High frequency words: a neglected resource for young literacy learners', the focus is on the hundred most common words in written English; these account for 50% of the total words in written English. How children's interest in these can be stimulated in a variety of ways is discussed. This chapter is based on an article in *Reading News*, published in 2013. This adapted version is included here with permission from the copyright holder, The Reading Association of Ireland.

Chapter 10, 'Reading and writing: a reciprocal relationship', is also adapted from *Young Literacy Learners: how we can help them*, where chapter 10 is devoted to a discussion of the value of stories read and re read to children in stimulating their understanding of written language. The stories drawn on as examples were all about 500 words in length, written by well-known children's authors for a Granada television series *Time for a Story,* for which I was one of two consultants. A number of illustrations are included to show the wide range of competence within a single class of children.

Chapter 6
Literacy Learning in Creative Contexts

This chapter is developed from a paper delivered at the Fourth International Congress for the Study of Child Language in Lund, Sweden in 1987, later published in *Children's Creative Communication*, R. Söderbergh (ed), 1988: 103-109.

Introduction

My interest in research in reading first developed during my experience as a primary school teacher of children aged seven and eight years of age, a large class with a wide range of ability and competence in reading. A desire to provide new insights of practical relevance has determined the precise formulation of the research issues on reading I have investigated, and subsequently other topics concerned with language development in young children.

Following the completion of my research projects I have attempted to stimulate in my students, many themselves experienced teachers, an interest in research. That is not itself sufficient. What has been important is that through practical assignments, based on my research and that of others, the students have been challenged to observe children sensitively in a variety of settings, in the expectation that this will make them more aware of the creativity of young children, actively seeking to make sense of their environment. It is hoped, these insights will lead them in turn to plan learning environments in school that support and extend the children's learning, and their search for meaning in the world around them. Young children are already involved in seeking such meanings before entry to school. In a print-filled environment this will include written language.

Readiness and Reading

There is plenty of evidence that young children in a print-filled, and literate environment are already, on entry to school, forming hypotheses about the print around them, some too limited, others too general, but all legitimate based on their current experience. They are developing some idea of both the functions and features of print. Some children enter school with their ideas already well-developed, ready to read, on the verge of reading, needing only further time to consolidate their experiences. Others have a long way to go; they need support, a variety of other experiences, including of print in a range of settings. This will enable them to master language in this new and more disembedded medium.

> What is now inevitably lacking is the familiar sense of ongoing purpose which informs nearly all normal conversation. These considerations make it very clear that tackling of print calls for quite new modes of thought and new kinds of interpretation. Print is essentially disembedded. (Donaldson and Reid, 1985:17)

There are several purposes for which written language is the medium of communication. Environmental print in the form of signs, and information textbooks with their own layout and conventions are two sources of written language. Narrative texts are a very different type of written language from environmental print. Stories have a continuous theme, an introduction, implicit rather than explicit connectedness, and resolution or ending. Non-fiction has a very different format from narrative text, requiring additional skills if children are to appreciate the implications of the layout, for example, columns, different sizes of font and diagrams contributing to the meaning. Each type of written language requires its own strategies and insights on the part of the child, each has its own place in the cognitive, linguistic and creative development of the child (see Blank, 1985 and Donaldson and Reid, 1985)

Lessons from Young Fluent Readers

My study of Young Fluent Readers (Clark 1976 and 1984) was planned to assess the strengths in these young children already reading fluently on entry to school, and the characteristics of their homes. Equally important was a consideration of weaknesses some of which might have been considered as leading inevitably to difficulty in learning to read and write; yet in spite of which they had been so precocious in their development.

Their strengths were not confined to reading, most of the children were already showing some awareness of how to represent words in written form. They knew what they could spell, and what they did not know, and their errors showed evidence of knowledge of the sequential probabilities in English spelling (Clark 1984). They showed both interest in and impressive competence in a wide variety of language tasks. It was interesting to note the way they read, which for most was silently, and the wide variety of purposes for which they read, for information in addition to pleasure.

There were a number of important findings from this study, not least caution against assuming an inevitable causal relationship between features of a child, or his or her environment, and progress in learning to read and write. See chapters 4 and 5 for more detail on these two studies.

Developing Awareness of Print

It is easy to dismiss outstanding children such as these. Some, though not all, were indeed gifted intellectually. It is important, however, to ensure that any conception of reading instruction and its essential features one holds can contain such children. Insights are now to be found from case studies of young preschool children on the ways that they develop awareness of the functions and features of written language, for example, when interacting in a story reading setting with their parents. There is also evidence of the importance of experiences of being read to for children's vocabulary, cognitive development, and later success in acquiring literacy. Two contrasting case studies are of interest in this connection. Bissex (1980 and 1984), studied her son Paul as he developed a keen awareness of the features of written language and increasing competence in its utilization for a variety of communicative purposes. Initially Paul`s interest was in communicating in writing rather than reading, hence the title of her book *GNYS AT WRK.* Butler (1975) reports vividly and with great insight the development of her severely handicapped granddaughter Cushla whose preschool development was greatly enriched by story reading and sharing, to quote:

It seems clear that access to a wealth of words and pictures, in a setting of consistent love and support has contributed enormously to her cognitive development in general and her language development in particular..... But perhaps, most of all, Cushla's books have surrounded her with friends; with people and warmth and colour during the days when her life was lived in almost constant pain and frustration. (Butler, 1975: 102)

Utilizing the case study approaches of Bissex and Butler and the insights provided in the empirical studies of Ferreiro (1982 and 1985), Payton, a student of mine, recorded story reading sessions with her young daughter and studied also Cecilia's growing appreciation of the features and functions of print (Payton, 1984). Children such as Cecilia may not be reading on entry to school, but they will require only a short time, patience and some further experience of print and they will perhaps quickly appear as a success of the school! Other children from less stimulating preschool settings, or homes where written language is less of a focus for the interactions that do take place, may require more patience, further stimulation, and a variety of other experiences.

Language and Literacy

It is interesting to speculate why story reading to a child, presenting as it does written language in oral form to the child in an interactional setting, should provide such a valuable stimulus to reading and the production of meaningful, interesting written language by the child. This is discussed further in chapter 10. A study of the text of the most effective and popular writers for children gives some insight into the contribution of such experiences to children's written language development. Anything more than a superficial glance reveals that such stories are not only a rich source of language, but also present subtle, continuous themes with much implicit as well as explicit meaning, with humour, and play on words. Much of importance is either not stated, or understated, and there is often rich direct speech as the characters interact with each other.

It is so often assumed that children with reading difficulties only have difficulties in reading. Thus any remedial attention they receive is directed specifically to this aspect. That they have difficulty in reading is not in dispute. For differential diagnosis, however, it is important to ascertain whether they can even understand and appreciate written language in an oral reading context. If they can, then it is legitimate to assume that their difficulty is specific, and to deal with it accordingly. Many such children, however, show a lack of ability to separate theme from description, the essential from the peripheral. For such children orally presented stories may be a valuable means for helping them to develop such skills. Not all backward readers fail to pay attention to detail; some do indeed concentrate on detail, but on aspects that are irrelevant for the task of reading. They do not separate the essential from the inessential, identify, but do not discriminate the critical features which distinguish one word or sentence from another.

The extent to which a child, for example an older backward reader, can retell with clarity a short story in written form to someone who does not know it, retaining the themes and essence of the original, is a valuable diagnostic measure. Further insights can be gained from observing the extent to which the child has understood the theme, and in oral retelling retains the style and language of the original. We found fascinating examples of this in many young preschool children after they had requested and had the same story read to them a number of times. To be asked to retell the story to an already well-informed adult as a comprehension task does not stimulate a child. Such a setting encourages the child to be vague, brief, providing only minimal information. Children from some homes succeed in such `educational games`, knowing how to humour the adults asking the questions. When children can retell orally presented written language vividly and with precision, they have achieved one important skill on the way to producing written language of quality. The writing of some older children with reading difficulties and with limited experience of reading a variety of written language shows few of the features of written language, and is little more than speech written down (see chapter 8).

Literacy Learning

To be creative, children must be able to utilize their experiences to produce written language which, while owing much to the experiences so far encountered, goes beyond these in expression and ideas. The challenge for us as researchers is to identify the crucial features in experiences which stimulate such creativity. For teachers, the challenge is to provide in education conditions that enable most children to achieve what a few already are developing, through a combination of their own characteristics and the stimulation they receive from those with whom they interact.

I recently discovered an article by Söderbergh, at whose conference in Lund I had given the paper on which this chapter is based (Söderbergh, 1998). It links closely with my discussion in chapter 10 on the relationship between reading and writing. This five-year-old fluent reader had amassed a large collection of drawings, illustrating episodes from stories she had read, most drawn four months to two years later, on occasion after she had reread the stories. The content of these is analysed in the article.

References

Bissex. G. L. (1980) *GNYS AT WRK: a child learns to read and write.* Cambridge, Mass: Harvard University Press.

Bissex, G. L. (1984) `The Child as Teacher`. In H. Goelman, A. Oberg, and F. Smith (eds), *Awakening to Literacy*. London: Heinemann Educational: 87-101.

Blank. M. (1985) `Language and School Failure: some speculations about the relationship between oral and written language`. In M. M. Clark (ed) *New Directions in the Study of Reading.* London: Palmer Press: 26-40.

Butler, D. (1975) *Cushla and her Books.* London: Heinemann Educational.

Clark, M. M. (1976) *Young Fluent Readers: what can they teach us?* London: Heinemann Educational.

Clark. M. M. (1979) *Reading Difficulties in Schools.* London: Heinemann Educational.

Clark, M. M. (1984) `Literacy at Home and at School: insights from a study of young fluent readers`. In H. Goelman, A. Oberg, A. and F. Smith (eds) *Awakening to Literacy.* London: Heinemann Educational: 122-130.

Clark, M. M. (ed) (1985) *New Directions in the Study of Reading.* London: Falmer Press.

Donaldson, M. and Reid. J. (1985) `Language Skills and Reading: a developmental perspective`. In M. M. Clark (ed) *New Directions in the Study of Reading.* London: Falmer Press: 12-25.

Ferreiro. E. and Teberosky, A. (1982) *Literacy Before Schooling.* Heinemann Educational, (UK Translation 1983).

Ferreiro, E. (1985) `The Relationship Between Oral and Written Language: the children's viewpoint`. In M. M. Clark (ed) *New Directions in the Study of Reading.* London: Falmer Press: 83-94.

Payton, S. (1984) *Developing Awareness of Print,* Birmingham: University of Birmingham: Educational Review. Offset Publication 2.

Söderbergh. R. (1998) `Narrative structure in drawings illustrating story texts by a five- and-a-half-year old fluent reader`, *Psychology of Language and Communication.* Vol. 2 (1): 17-36.

Chapter 7
Sensitive Observation and the Development of Literacy: a tribute to Marie Clay

This chapter is based on an article in *Literacy Today,* September 2007: 12-13, an updated version of an article in *Educational Psychology* 1992, 12, 3: 215-223. It was written on the occasion of Marie Clay's death in 2007. There is further information on Reading Recovery, in an article titled 'Reading recovery rediscovery' also in *Literacy Today*, March 2007.

Background

This chapter is a personal tribute to Dame Marie Clay who died in April 2007. She was made a Dame of the British Empire in 1987 and named New Zealander of the Year in 1994. She was awarded honorary degrees by five overseas universities and was the author of 32 books. Tributes to her contribution to early literacy have been paid around the world. I first met Marie in the early 1970s at a conference in Copenhagen, and shortly afterwards was invited by Marie to spend a term in Auckland University.

Self-correction in young children

Marie Clay's contribution to our understanding of the development of literacy in young children has long been internationally recognised. Perhaps it was her grounding in developmental psychology that led her to undertake her pioneering work on close observations of young children in the early stages of learning to read. The first article in which she reported her comparisons of the errors and self-correction of children making high and low progress in the early stages of learning to read was published in 1969. At the time I met Marie Clay, when she was reporting these results, I was involved in research into children who were already reading with fluency and understanding when they came to school at five years of age, some from homes where no one would have had such expectations (Clark, 1976). Marie and I therefore had a great deal in common and during the three months I spent in Auckland University in the early 1970s I was able to observe the impact she already had on the teaching of reading throughout New Zealand, in particular on the identification and remediation of reading difficulties early in a young child`s career, before the failure was ingrained.

Reading, a patterning of complex behaviour

Within a few years Reading Recovery, with its running records and other diagnostic instruments, had been adopted in many States in Australia and in parts of the United States. Reading Recovery programmes were being enthusiastically adopted in a number of local authorities in the United Kingdom, with support from Marie Clay herself and tutors from New Zealand. Only the withdrawal of funding gradually led to the disappearance of many of these programmes in England. There remain a number of well-trained teachers with greater insight into the complexity of the development of literacy and how to diagnose the needs of young children, who benefited from that training.

More recently, with great publicity, an initiative was heralded on television, which it was claimed, though expensive, was valuable in helping to identify and support young children before literacy failure was ingrained. I watched the programme and the tributes from one head teacher who had adopted the approach. To my astonishment the programme was referred to as Reading Recovery, with, however, no mention of its origin in New Zealand, or in 1970s! (see `Reading Recovery rediscovery,` Clark 2007). A recent publication, *Reading Recovery and Every Child a Reader: history, policy and practice,* (Burroughs-Lange and Ince, 2013) traces the history of these developments. In that publication, in chapter 1, Douëtil, Hobsbaum and Maidment trace the development of Reading Recovery in England from 1990-2005, across the UK and in the Republic of Ireland. In chapter 2 the further development linked with Every Child a Reader is discussed.

By 1972 Marie had published her first book on literacy, *Reading: the patterning of complex behaviour,* followed in 1991 by a second edition again with a title reflecting her appreciation of the complexity of literacy development, *Becoming Literate: the construction of inner control* (Clay 1972 and 1991). She combined with a theoretical basis practical insights that encouraged practitioners to make close observations of children. Her 'running records', gradually adopted as a means of diagnostic assessment of children's oral reading, replaced some of the rather sterile oral reading tests. Her 'concepts of print', adopted by many teachers, has led to a greater appreciation of the range of competence within even a single group of children on entry to school (Clay, 1979).

For many years there had been, and still are, controversies about the best method of teaching reading, with battle lines drawn between phonics advocates (currently synthetic phonics taking priority in England) and those who favour other methods at the early stages. Marie Clay avoided being drawn into these sterile arguments and stressed the need for appreciating that, whatever approach is adopted, there will be casualties; the problems will be different. She noted the importance of observing the strategies of high progress children, including their errors, and those not explicitly stressed within the method adopted for their initial instruction. Low progress children she felt may then require more explicit guidance.

The history of developments in the study of literacy is studded with references to the work of Marie Clay. When others were looking on reading as a purely visual skill to be acquired by didactic teaching, Marie was referring to it as 'a patterning of complex behaviour' (Clay 1972). It is a tribute to Marie that throughout her long association with the field of reading she never allowed herself to be aligned with one 'camp', as she herself stated, she found:

> the big debates divisive, for people feel obliged to take up opposing positions on matters like phonological awareness, the reader's use of context, and the nature of getting meaning from texts. (Clay, 1991: 3)

It is worth noting, particularly in the present climate, the reason she gave for not writing anything on methodology. She felt that the underlying structure of literacy behaviours might be achieved in several different ways, and that successful readers and writers emerge from many different types of programmes. She made a plea we recognise that:

> *some children need extra resources and many more supportive interactions with teachers* to get them through the necessary transitions of reading acquisition to the stage where they can pick up most of the different kinds of information in print. (Italics in the original: Clay, 1991: 345)

Case studies of individual children

By 1980s there was already a growing awareness of insights that could be gained from case studies of individual children, including observations of their earliest interactions with print in the home prior to starting school, not only in books, but also of environmental print. These studies revealed just how wide might be the range of understanding of concepts of print on entry to school, even within a single class, something to which insufficient appreciation had been given previously. Glenda Bissex, for example, studied her own son's development where his interest in writing preceded his reading development (Bissex, 1980). Dorothy Butler, one of Marie Clay's students, for her dissertation studied her pre-school handicapped granddaughter Cushla's interactions with books and stories. Again there was a parallel with my own interests, as one of my students, Shirley Payton, made a close observation of her pre-school daughter's earliest interactions with stories and written language. Marie, like me, was concerned as to whether the student could remain sufficiently objective to undertake such a study; to our relief both students were able to capitalize on these experiences, providing new insights from these close observations (Butler, 1979; Payton, 1984). Later, Clay and Butler collaborated on further books with a focus on the important role played by the home in establishing the foundations of literacy. (*Reading Begins at Home,* Butler and Clay, 1979)

The reciprocal relationship between writing and reading

In 1980 Marie Clay presented a paper at a symposium in Birmingham in which she considered the reciprocal relationship between reading and writing. She drew attention to the benefit of the analytic tasks associated with writing in facilitating reading, not only in high progress children, but also in less competent children. At that time practice in writing, other than possibly handwriting, was so often delayed until children had acquired competence in reading. Marie Clay stressed the value of the writing component in the programme she was developing for children who, after a year of reading instruction, were not making progress (`Early writing and reading: reciprocal gains`, Clay, 1980).

Any new directions in the teaching of literacy and assessment of reading progress must not lose sight of Marie Clay`s claim, backed with empirical evidence, that children can be active and creative in their search for meaning, if the situations we provide enable them to engage in such explorations. It is to be hoped that any move towards `the basics` is not `back to the basics`, if by that we risk ignoring the findings of creative researchers and teachers such as Marie Clay.

References

Bissex, G. L. (1980) *GNYS AT WRK: a child learns to write and read.* Cambridge, MA: Harvard University Press.

Burroughs-Lange, S. and Ince, A. (eds) (2013) *Reading Recovery and Every Child a Reader: history, policy and practice.* London: IOE Press.

Butler, D. (1979) *Cushla and her Books.* Auckland: Hodder and Stoughton.

Butler, D. and Clay, M. (1979) *Reading Begins at Home.* Auckland, Heinemann Educational.

Clark, M. M. (1976) *Young Fluent Readers: what can they teach us?* London: Heinemann Educational.

Clark, M. M. (1992) `Sensitive observation and the development of literacy`. *Educational Psychology*, 12, 3: 215-223.

Clark, M. M. (2007a) `Reading Recovery rediscovery`, *Literacy Today* March: 8.

Clark, M. M. (2007b) `Sensitive observation and the development of literacy: a tribute to Marie Clay`, *Literacy Today*, September: 12-13.

Clay, M. M. (1969) `Reading errors and self-correction behaviour`. *British Journal of Educational Psychology* 39, 1: 47-56.

Clay, M. M. (1972) *Reading: the patterning of complex behaviour.* Auckland: Heinemann Educational.

Clay, M. M. (1979) *The Early Detection of Reading Difficulties: a diagnostic survey with recovery procedures.* Auckland: Heinemann Educational.

Clay, M. M. (1980) `Early writing and reading: reciprocal gains`. In M. M. Clark and T. Glynn (eds) *Reading and Writing for the Child with Difficulties.* Occ. Pub. 8: 27-43. University of Birmingham. Educational Review.

Clay, M. M. (1991) *Becoming Literate: the construction of inner control.* Auckland, Heinemann Educational.

Douëtil, J. Hobsbaum, A. and Maidment, P. (2013) `Reading Recovery, an early literacy intervention`. In S. Burroughs-Lande and A. Ince (eds) *Reading Recovery and Every Child a Reader: history, policy and practice.* London: IOE Press: 5-37.

Payton, S. (1984) *Developing Awareness of Print*. Offset Pub 2 University of Birmingham, Educational Review.

Chapter 8
Meeting Individual Needs in Learning to Read

In an article of mine with the title 'Reading in the Balance', in *Child Education,* October 1993: 31-55, there was a subtitle, 'Can we hold on to the best innovations of recent years and meet the new English requirements for reading? A similar issue arises at the present time. That article led to a commission from Scholastic to extend the article to a book. *Young Literacy Learners: how we can help them,* (1994). There, research references supporting the approaches described in this chapter are to be found.

Outline

In this chapter I discuss briefly five aspects of importance in enabling young children to learn to read and write in a creative environment. I developed many of these ideas when I worked as a volunteer in an inner city school, deliberately avoiding the use of expensive resources, to set an example of what could be achieved on a limited budget. Some of the children's illustrations are from the class of seven and eight-year-olds with whom I worked. Other illustrations were brought either by my students, or teachers with whom I worked. Further ideas are to be found in the following two chapters.

A crucial starting point for all teachers of young children should be to observe each child's responses and attempts at reading and writing in a variety of stimulating activities, working in partnership with parents to give further insights. To any literate adult the relationship between spoken and written language may seem obvious. Children have to be helped to discover this relationship. We must remember that to a beginner, the differences between words, letters, punctuation marks and numbers may not be obvious. Phonics instruction related to written words may be meaningless to young children who are not yet able to hear the constituent sounds in spoken language. To read for meaning and enjoyment children need to be able to use a variety of strategies to recognise speedily and automatically high frequency words. They may also need direct instruction on word analysis in context.

Encouragement and stimulation of young children's attempts to read and write is important, including with their invented spellings, then moving forward to conventional spelling of an increasing range of familiar words. Children will be stimulated to gain meaning from print if from the earliest stages they are made aware of a wide range of meaningful reading material, including environmental print, narrative and information text.

In this chapter illustrations are given of contexts within which young children's awareness of written language can be developed. Researches are not cited here to back up the statements. However, they have arisen from knowledge of a wide range of research and these are referenced in *Young Literacy Learners* (Clark, 1994) and were discussed here in Section I.

This chapter is in five sections:

- Concepts of print, what children bring from home;
- stories as a first step, developing language for literacy;
- linking sounds to writing, auditory discrimination of sounds in words;
- phonics with a purpose, learning the alphabet and word analysis;
- real reading, supporting beginners and more confident readers.

The order of the sections is not intended to suggest that these should be treated either in sequence or in isolation. The level at which individual children can participate with any aspect will depend on their entry skills and previous experience. Speedy recognition of high frequency words in context is important if children are to read with understanding. Why teach children to recognise words as wholes? Twelve words make up about a quarter of the total of words in print (a, and, he, I, in, is, it, of, that the, to, was). Ways of helping children acquire this ability will be discussed further in chapter 9. While the hundred key words account for about 50 per cent of the *total* words in written language, words that appear less frequently account for 90 per cent of the *different* words. To become independent readers and writers children need also to develop strategies for the speedy identification of words that occur less frequently and words they are meeting for the first time. In chapter 10, consideration will be given to the reciprocal relationship between reading and writing and ways to help children become creative in their written language through the medium of stories.

Concepts of print

Concepts of print are already familiar to some young children, even in pre-school, who may know most of the letters of the alphabet, be able to write their own name and perhaps a few other words. Some believe they can already read and write when doing pretend writing or retelling a favourite story with a book in their hands. A few children enter school already able to read with understanding and enjoyment, without having had any explicit tuition. In the same class there may be children who are not yet aware of the difference between drawing and writing, are unable to write their own name and who know none of the letters of the alphabet.

Suggestion:

- Check for each child whether you can recognise their drawings; whether any of their writing is meaningful; whether there are any real words, guessable words, letter-like forms or just scribbles to represent writing. Keep a folder for each child to enable you to monitor their progress and encourage parents to add examples.

The illustrations below show young children, some pre-school, with different levels of concepts of print. They are taken from my time as a volunteer in an inner city school where I had no resources to purchase materials, and from courses I conducted with teachers where they were encouraged to bring examples from their classes.

The first illustrations are from *Young Literacy Learners* page 36 and show the very different levels of concepts of print in six pre-school children.

Ben (3 years, 5 months)

'Writing about my brother.'

Kirsty (3 years, 4 months)

(with other similar figures)

'It says my family.'

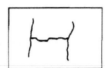

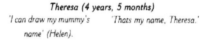

Theresa (4 years, 5 months)

'I can draw my mummy's name' (Helen).

'Thats my name, Theresa.'

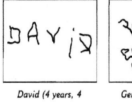

David (4 years, 4 months)

Gemma (4 years, 4 months)

'It says, for my mum.'

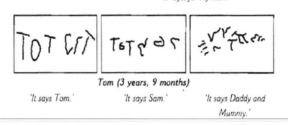

Tom (3 years, 9 months)

'It says Tom.'

'It says Sam.'

'It says Daddy and Mummy.'

Figure 1 Concepts of print in pre-school children

The following examples are from two girls, both aged 4 years 9 months, showing their very different understanding of written language.

Hannah (4 years, 9 months)

Sharleen (4 years, 9 months)

Figure 2 Understanding of concepts of print by two children aged 4 years 9 months

Some children believe something is for reading if it has several different symbols. Some young children may in their attempts at writing incorporate letters from their name in their pretend writing. See *Awakening to Literacy*, H. Goelman, A. Oberg and F. Smith (eds) (1984), in particular chapters by Bissex, Ferreiro, Y. Goodman and Clark. The contribution of Marie Clay to sensitive monitoring of children's developing awareness of print is discussed here in the previous chapter, Chapter 7.

Stories as a first step

Through stories children come to experience a wide vocabulary, and in context. They hear words and phrases that seldom occur in spoken language, thus sensitizing them to features of written language. Young children who have wide experience of stories read to them often use expressions from favourite stories in their spoken language, for example in retelling a story. Through stories children can be helped to hear the conventions of grammatically correct English. Those who have many stories read to them often want to write their own stories on a similar theme. Children who have had a rich fund of stories read to them, even very young children, may simulate `book language` when pretending to read or retelling the story; indeed they may adopt the author`s style, even when not exactly reproducing what was on the page. The following extract is from a three-year-old boy, Barrie. As he read he insisted on having the book in front of him, the pages of which he turned dramatically, and during the reading he used a special voice, interspersed with asides using colloquial speech. The recording was made in a nursery school as early as 1970s as part of an observational research into interest in books and stories This extract is from page 52 in *Young Literacy Learners* (Clark, 1994).

Child
"They`re just ordinary beans", said Jack.

"They`re magic beans just plant them in the garden and they will grow".

"How did you know my name", said Jack.

Book

"I would be a fool to exchange my cow for your beans", said Jack.

"Ah! But these are not ordinary beans", replied the butcher, "they are magic beans".

Jack was amazed that she knew his name.

The observational study in a nursery school was originally published as early as 1979 in chapter 6 by Carol Lomax in *Studies in Pre-school Education,* M. M. Clark and W.M. Cheyne (eds). Many strategies were observed as some of the young children made sure that the story read was their choice; that their favourite story was reread to them. On one occasion a child asked the nursery nurse to `read it`, when she began to tell a story with which he was familiar. The children frequently spoke to themselves or their friends in the manner of someone reading as they looked through books in the book corner. This pretend reading was quite different in delivery and style from interspersed comments about the story. While pictures were sometimes a stimulus, it is worth noting that one child reported excitedly to her friends that they were about to have a story without pictures. It was unusual in that nursery school to see even the younger children, only three years of age, looking at a book the wrong way up or going through the pages in the wrong direction. This was one of the first nursery schools to be opened in that county, and it should be noted was in a very deprived area. The head teacher was committed to encouraging a love of print and had requested that we include this observational study in our research, which was on the invitation of the director of education. There was even a library in the nursery school which these young pre-children helped to run and from which they could borrow books to take home.

Three early interesting references with ideas for developing a love of written language are the following:

Cushla and her Books, D. Butler (1979) Auckland: Hodder and Stoughton.

The Foundations of Literacy, D. Holdaway (1979) Sydney: Ashton Scholastic.

Wally`s Stories, V. G. Paley (1981) Cambridge, Mass: Harvard University Press.

See chapter 10 in this current book for a more extended discussion of the reciprocal relationship between reading and writing.

Linking sounds to writing

There is a relationship between the meaningful words we speak and the groups of symbols on paper in written language. The words we speak can be broken down into their component parts of individual phonemes and syllables. A phoneme is the smallest unit of sound that can change the meaning of a word. Researchers have shown how important phonemic awareness is for learning to read, the ability to break a word into its component parts. Children who have difficulty can be helped to acquire this skill. Word games and those that involve rhyme and alliteration can help, also experience of breaking words into segments which have common elements.

Children who are good at reading and spelling are good at identifying rhyme and alliteration. Some activities require knowledge of the alphabet and most children when they come to school know the names of some of the letters; these can be the starting point. Games can help children acquire, or extend their knowledge of the alphabet and make for speedy recognition. Children's invented spellings seem to sharpen their appreciation of the structure of words. As children gain more appreciation their attention should be drawn to correct spellings, initially of words they use frequently.

Suggestions:

- I spy or cards with several pictures of words starting with the same sound;
- initial sounds in the children's own name can be a stimulus;
- spotting the rhymes in nursery rhymes and poems can be fun;
- thinking up words that rhyme is also helpful;
- spotting errors in well-known rhymes can be fun;
- searching for words within words helps.

See *Rhyme and Reason in Reading and Spelling,* L. Bradley and P. Bryant (1985), University of Michigan Press.

Phonics with a purpose

The high frequency words account for half the *total* words in print; however, they account for only a tiny proportion of the *different* words in print. These remaining 90 per cent of words will be met much less frequently, but need to be recognised speedily to help reading comprehension. For this reason children need to employ a range of strategies, including whole word recognition, decoding and contextual cues. They need to acquire a speedy and reliable recognition of the letters of the alphabet if they are to tackle unfamiliar words and appreciate the relationship between the sounds they utter and the marks on paper. Children need to know both the names and the sounds of the letters; to be able to differentiate letters one from another, and the difference between punctuation marks and letters. In short, they need to appreciate the critical features in written language. Capital letter recognition is as important as lower case, as most environmental print is in capital letters. Furthermore, their distinctiveness is easily recognised, they can be more irregular and still recognisable. In my research into young fluent readers (*Young Fluent Readers; what can they teach us?* 1976) I found that many of these children preferred to use capital letters in their writing. It is worth noting that more than one third of lower case letters depend for their distinctiveness on position in space and therefore may be more easily confused and more difficult to recognise if badly formed (n, u, h, y, m, w, b, d, p, q for example). The aim of phonics is to enable children to develop a working knowledge of the sound symbol relationship and the probable spelling patterns in English. From this they can:

- Recognise an unfamiliar word quickly;
- tackle words by splitting them into syllables which they can identify;
- spot shorter words within long words.

Some children do acquire those skills from their extensive experience with stories and word and letter games they play before they come to school. For other children direct instruction is critically important if they are to become independent readers and writers. However, the extent to which children will use their phonics instruction depends on the degree to which they have found it useful in recognition of words in their earliest written texts. A planned programme of phonics instruction should as far as possible use comparison between words, and words in meaningful sentences. See chapters 14-18 for further discussion on phonics in the teaching of reading.

Suggestions:

- Make an alphabet book with children choosing illustrations for the letters. More advanced children may want to look up words in a dictionary;
- working in groups children could form sentences with each word starting with the same letter;
- tongue twisters or spells are fun;
- they might find out how many words they can make using only the letters from a particular word. One pair of children with whom I worked managed to make 17 words from the word `question`.

These activities can help to link spoken words with their written representation. Figure 3 is an illustration of tongue twisters from *Young Literacy Learners*: 101. The originals were all brightly coloured.

Figure 3 Examples of tongue twisters from 7-8 year-old children

Real reading and writing

All the following types of reading give purpose to young children's early experiences of print.

Public or environmental print: Signs, labels and advertisements. These are the least disembedded of any written language;

Information text: This can start with very simple instructions with illustrations, perhaps on computers, for example how to look after a pet, play a game, assemble a toy or draw up a shopping list. Some children prefer this to stories.

Faction books: These are books that deal with true events but describe them using the techniques of fiction. While non-fiction books interest some children, faction books can be a valuable bridge between narrative texts and non-fiction. Mogens Jansen, in Denmark, wrote a series of 25 little green faction books in Danish about 40 years ago, with historically correct photographs or drawings; the content was checked by experts for accuracy; each book was about 32 pages in length. The books, retaining the illustrations, were translated into many other languages. The criteria for these as for other books were:

- Whether the book is worth reading;
- whether the language is accessible;
- whether the concepts are clear for the reader;
- whether the facts are accurate.

I am grateful to Mogens Jansen for this information.

Narrative text: Rhymes, short stories with plenty of repetition and direct speech are popular. These real books should be distinguished from scheme readers devised for the purpose of reading instruction. It is important to prepare children sufficiently and not teach on the book so that they can gain meaning from the text and enjoy the written word. Even competent adult readers find it difficult to read with understanding if they read too slowly.

Suggestions:

- Read part of a sentence pausing for the children to take part, using a book with which the children are already familiar.
- Consider the purpose of oral reading by the child, for some children pausing long enough for the child to self-correct. For other children it may be better to supply the problem word to retain enough speed for meaningful reading.
- Ensure that the book is of the correct level of difficulty so that it will be a challenge, but that the child has sufficient strategies to gain meaning and enjoyment. This is where the running records are a valuable tool (see Chapter 7).

- Encourage children to read silently then retell the story, but to someone who is not familiar with it, so that there is meaning in the retelling.
- Ensure that the children have a broad experience of books and that you are sensitive to the needs of the children whose reading level is more advanced.

Insights into the complexities of the English language

The teacher is not the only source of help for children learning to read. Tape recordings, computers, and environmental print can extend the children's experience of print. Other children can help their classmates; school and local libraries can widen the available resources. Parents and other adults can continue to be a valuable resource.

As a young girl I was fascinated by Lewis Carroll's *Alice's Adventures in Wonderland* (1865). On looking at that book again recently, and *Through the Looking Glass* (1872), I found there many insights into the subtleties of, and possibilities of play on words, in the English language. These books would repay study by practitioners, and children themselves, who might come to appreciate the possibility for fun in written English. There is only space here to remind readers of a few examples from each book:

Alice felt dreadfully puzzled. The Hatter's remark seemed to her to have no sort of meaning in it, and yet it was certainly English.

Take care of the sense and the sounds will take care of themselves.

'Of course you know your A B C', said the Red Queen.... 'I can even read words of one letter! ..... You'll come to that in time'.

'Twas brillig, and the slithy toves Did gyre and gimble in the wabe:

What fun to make sense of this, or better still make up your own version!

Chapter 9
High Frequency Words: a neglected resource in learning to read

This chapter is based on an article in *Reading News,* Sept. 2013: 15-17.

High frequency words: their contribution to reading

In this chapter I consider the value of including knowledge of the hundred commonest words in written English in helping children to become fluent readers. I suggest experiences that could give children a rich diet of written language in the early stages.

There are a number of reasons why we should spend time encouraging young children to recognise the commonest words in English in a variety of meaningful contexts.

- The relationship of words to spoken language is much easier for young children to grasp than the abstract concept of letters;
- relatively few words account for a high proportion of the total words in written as well as spoken English;
- some of the common words are not phonically regular;
- few of the most frequent words have meaning in isolation, most take their meaning from the words around them;
- these are not easily represented pictorially, as few are either nouns or verbs;
- these are likely to be influenced by the context.

What are the commonest words in written English? Based on research in 1960s McNally and Murray prepared a list of the commonest key words in written English. They claimed that these hundred words account for about half the total words in everyday reading material. It is worth noting that a further 100 words contribute only 10-15 per cent more of the words and beyond this it is a case of diminishing returns, as the type of reading material strongly influences the remaining words that appear frequently in a particular text. For further details of this, and ways in which young children can have fun experiencing such words from a variety of easily accessible reading materials see *Young Literacy Learners,* Clark, 1994: chapter 6.

In a recent article, Solity and Vousden (2009) analysed the structure of adult literature, children's real books and reading schemes and examined the demands they make on children's sight vocabulary and phonic skills. It is worth noting that these authors used the McNally and Murray 100 commonest word list from the 1960s in their analysis and still found it valuable. They claim that, `the debate may be resolved by teaching an optimal level of core phonological, phonic, and sight vocabulary skills, rigorously and systematically in conjunction with the use of real books`.(Solity and Vousden, 2009: 503)

The hundred key words

According to McNally and Murray the following twelve words account for about 25 per cent of the total words:

a and he I in is it of that the to was

The following twenty words account for about a further 10 per cent of the total words:

all as at be but are for had have him his not on one said so they we with you.

The following 68 words account for another 20 per cent of the total words:

about an back been before big by call came can come could did do down first from get go has her here if into just like little look made make me more much must my no new now off old only or our other out over right see she some their them then there this two when up want well went were what where which who will your.

Practical suggestions using readily available materials

Pages from old magazines, newspapers, duplicated stories or other examples of genuine written language are a useful resource on which children can make marks using different coloured pens. Two or more children can be given the same sample, and the same or different words to spot, then compare their findings. Progressively they can be given more words. Children love to show that they have spotted words that others have missed. This can easily be planned to meet the needs of individual children at different levels.

Provide the children with examples of written language with which they are already familiar such as nursery rhymes or short stories, and ask them to identify how many of the first twelve key words they contain, for example, the The THE or in different sizes of print. This enables them to become sensitized to the critical features of words, how the format, the colour or size can change without changing the word.

I used this word-hunt technique to great effect with young children aged seven or eight who could barely read, and children who had little grasp of English. I also used a duplicated version of a short story of about 500 words, *When the Moon Winked,* retold by Sara and Stephen Corrin, which I read to them several times. I have quoted below the first eight lines of the story, where I asked them to find how many times the first twelve key words appeared. These accounted for 28 of the 78 words.

> Once there was a king who wanted to touch the moon.
>
> This was the only thing he could think of,
>
> day and night, day and night. He even dreamt about it.
>
> "I must, I must, I really must touch the moon", he kept muttering.
>
> He called his Head carpenter to him.

"I've simply got to touch the moon", he told him,

"and your job will be to build me a tower that will reach up to the sky".

See chapter 10 for examples of children's versions of this story, several with illustrations.

A word count of short stories such as that cited above, revealed the value of speedy recognition of the commonest words. It was helpful also to point out the relationship between these words and for example is-isn't, it-it's, was-wasn't, I-I've, I'll, he-he'll, he's, that-that's, you-you'd. In many stories for children in real books (that is not in simplified language), there is a great deal of direct speech, and the children are likely to find many such words. It is important for the children to be aware that key words may be in capital letters, start with a capital or a lower case letter and still be the same word.

Learning the hundred key words can be valuable for children in the early stages of learning to read, making them more observant of written language in a variety of contexts. It can also be made fun. Some additional words may be guessed from the context by an experienced reader who is following the sense of the passage, or who has a grasp of the structure of English sentences. Some words, though not among the hundred key words, will appear repeatedly within a particular context, but infrequently elsewhere. The children's attention could be drawn to these words in advance. One child with whom I was working on the above story became excited and wanted also to count the words that were key words within that story. See chapter 10 for a more detailed discussion of the reciprocal relationship between spoken and written language.

Concluding comments

As was stressed in the previous chapter, while high frequency words account for about half the total words, it is essential to be able to recognise speedily also the words that appear much less frequently. These account for over 90 per cent of the *different* words in written language. For this reason children if they are to read with understanding need to develop strategies for speedy recognition of words they have not met before. It is with this latter aspect that a grasp of phonics will assist the children. However, there is evidence that this is better practised in context, not in isolation or as a part of commercial programmes as currently advocated in England (see chapter 14 for research evidence). Time spent in some schools on practising pseudo words in anticipation of the phonics check, as is happening in England, could surely be better spent studying the features of real written English. There are some schools where the home language of all, or the majority of children, is different from that used in school. Recent evidence shows that many children learn to read in their second language rather than their mother tongue. According to Deacon and Cain (2011) at least half the world's children learn to read in a second language. See chapters 20 and 21 for further discussion of this issue.

References

Clark, M. M. (1994) *Young Literacy Learners: how we can help them.* Leamington Spa: Scholastic.

Clark, M. M. (2013a) `Is there one best method of teaching reading? What is the evidence?` *Education Journal.* Issue 156: 14-16.*

Clark, M. M. (2013b) `The phonics check for all year 1 children in England: its background, results and possible effects`. *Education Journal.* Issue 160: 6-8.*

Clark, M. M. (2013c) `Research evidence on the first phonics check for all year 1 children in England: is it accurate and is it necessary?` *Education Journal.* Issue 168: 12-15.*

Deacon, H. and Cain, K. (2011) `What have we learnt from learning to read in more than one language`. *Journal of Research in Reading.* 34 (1): 1-5. This is a special issue on learning to read in more than one language.

Solity, J. and Vousden, J. (2009) `Real books vs reading schemes: a new perspective from instructional psychology`. *Educational Psychology*. Vol. 29 (4): 469-511.

*See chapters 14-16 for adapted versions of these articles.

Chapter 10
Reading and Writing: a reciprocal relationship

This chapter is adapted from *Young Literacy Learners: how we can help them* (Clark, 1994). The full text of two of the books from which illustrations are included here was in the appendix to that book. Granada Television gave permission for this, to allow teachers to make use of the ideas suggested in the teachers` booklets. The original texts are not repeated here, as some of the children`s versions give the flavour of the stories. The illustrations in this chapter have been scanned from the original publication, so unfortunately are not as clear as they might otherwise have been. Most of the originals were in colour.

Background

In this chapter I am adopting a more personal approach by focusing on ways that I and my students used short stories as a stimulus for young children`s reading and writing. The stories used illustratively were written by well-known children`s authors for *Time for a Story,* a television resource for developing literacy, broadcast by Granada Television between 1986 and 1988.Wendy Dewhirst and I were the consultants for the series, involved in helping with the planning of the programmes, and we prepared the teachers` notes. The story books, teachers` notes, audio tapes and the programmes are no longer available. However, I have continued to use a selection of the story books. These are used here to illustrate their value in early literacy development.

Outline of the series Time for a Story

The television series, *Time for a Story*, for children aged four to six years of age, was transmitted weekly on Granada Television between 1986 and 1988. There were twenty-eight programmes, each lasting ten minutes, each including a different short story. The narrator, Bill Oddie, set the scene for the story of about 500 words, read and reread extracts from the stories. Some stories needed introductory comments to set the scene, in other

91

instances more time was available for discussion following the reading. The children were encouraged later to compose their own stories, with language as complex as in these stories. The only constraint placed on the well-known authors submitting stories for consideration was that the story should be around 500 words in length. Most of the books were enlivened by direct speech between the characters. Little books, with the stories and illustrations from the programmes, audio tapes and the teachers` booklets could be purchased.

Unfortunately at that time there were only limited resources for recording programmes, and only in a few schools. Though some advisers made recordings available in teachers` centres many teachers only viewed the programmes live with the children and did not purchase the materials; thus they did not gain full benefit from the programmes. These constraints sadly limited the value of the programmes in some schools. However, I was able to use video recordings, and the materials in a number of schools, stimulating children to write their own stories on similar themes. In this chapter I have set out the rationale for using stories such as these with young children and some of the key points from the teachers` booklets.

The aim of this television series was to provide a rich variety of story themes and styles to extend the children`s experience of written English found in books, and encourage and stimulate those whose experiences have been more limited. The linked story and illustrations were also intended to help the younger children, and those whose language was less advanced to understand the text. The limited extracts of print from the stories shown on screen had a function also, even for the younger children not yet able to read all or many of the words in isolation. The sentences and phrases were said, and often repeated, by the presenter in a way that could help children's developing awareness of print. Clearly the medium of television cannot be a substitute for the dynamic interactions in story sessions at home, and often at school, nor can it in isolation teach children to read. However, new ideas can be illustrated through the medium of television, particularly backed by resources and follow-up activities setting these in context.

Key points from the programmes

Each programme was self-contained; however, children who watched the whole series experienced a wide range of story themes, with varied styles of written text, illustrations and of print-related activities. As the context for each story was established within the programme preliminary activities were not required. Teachers were not expected to participate during a programme, but to encourage the children to look and listen.

The stories were selected for their likely appeal to a wide range of children and to represent a variety of styles and topics. The language of the stories is varied as each author used their own style. The published books retain the text precisely as read on screen. As an aid to emphasis and meaning, the conventions of punctuation, and variation in type of print used in these books, and many children's books, was retained on screen. These included speech marks, exclamation marks, question marks and capital letters for emphasis.

It was not possible for the children to ask questions or seek clarification during the story reading as would be natural if the setting were a parent and child together, or a small group or class with their teacher. For this reason key concepts were introduced in anticipation, if essential to the understanding and enjoyment of the story. For other stories, anticipation and surprise are ingredients of the story. Each story was supported by vivid illustrations, in a variety of styles, representing important concepts and incidents in the story. The illustrations were prepared for television, but not by the authors, some of whom would normally have illustrated their own books. The illustrations heightened the children's enjoyment and enabled stories to be understood even by children who might find the text in isolation rather complex. A few selected illustrations were incorporated in the little books.

The combination of text with rich dialogue and the illustrations, was intended to enable the stories to be enjoyed at their own level by younger children, those with less advanced language skills, limited knowledge of English, or limited experience of the language of story books and of print.

There were, in addition, sufficient subtleties of meaning and language to stimulate, interest and challenge the more advanced and any child who could already read with fluency and understanding.

Children are entitled to their own views and preferences which should be encouraged and cultivated. They come to anticipate some of the rich dialogue in stories such as these and the precise words of the original. It was not expected, or intended that the younger children would be able to read much of the text on screen. The text and illustrations in the stories in the television series were normally complementary, but on occasion in stories the text can stand alone, leaving the illustrations to the child's imagination. In picture books, particularly for young children, the 'message' may be carried by a combination of illustrations and words, on occasion both from the same hand. Children may subsequently create stories themselves on similar themes in either written or spoken language, or by drawing and painting, depending on their chosen medium for communication and present level of competence.

Follow-up and extension activities were suggested in the notes to each programme. These might include re-reading and retelling these stories and similar stories by the teacher, other stories and poems on similar themes; illustrations of the events of the stories in sequence drawn by individual children, or groups of children co-operating in retelling the story through that medium. This activity is pleasurable in its own right and also one that helps children to grasp key incidents in the story.

In the teachers' booklets information was provided about the vocabulary used in the stories, its extent and similarity and a note of some of the key words in the individual stories. Subsequently I used some of these stories and ideas in courses for teachers and in classrooms with young children.

Developing sensitivity to spoken and written language

Children gradually become aware of written language as a medium of communication and that a read story, in contrast to a told story, will remain the same, not only in theme but also in language. They come to realize that the print, not the pictures, are what is read, although they come to appreciate that the pictures may help to explain the text. Children come to realize that printed language can exist and carry meaning in the absence of pictures, and it does not label or even merely describe pictures. They are well aware that a read story is of a finite length, and will indeed often object strongly if an attempt is made to omit any of it on a re-reading. Gradually children become sensitive to the relative implications of particular expressions and their relationship to the stage in the narrative. A similar sentence near the beginning or near the end of a story may, for example, have a different significance.

The reciprocal relationship between reading and writing and the way in which each can help and support the other was already being stressed in 1980s. Case studies revealed how sensitive to this were many children, even pre-school children. (see chapter 8)

Stimulating children`s drawing and writing of stories

Illustrating and retelling stories

There are many examples in *Young Literacy Learners* of children`s writing, from reception class to seven or eight years of age, based on stories read to them. On pages 66 and 67 there are four examples of retelling of *The Three Little Pigs* by children in reception class (five years of age), ranging from a child who cannot yet write any words to a girl who loves writing. Although some of the words in her version are in invented rather than correct English spelling, it is possible to read her story.

Over the period when the television series *Time for a Story* was being developed and transmitted, my students were able to use the ideas as a basis for practical work with children of a wide age range; later we used the little books written for the series. Over the following ten years I continued to make use of the more effective stories with a wide age range of children; only a few examples could be included here. I showed the television programme of *When the Moon Winked* in a primary school in Singapore committed to the value of books and stories from the earliest stage. The children saw the programme only once and did not have the books. The following day, before I left Singapore, I was presented with a folder of fascinating versions of the story beautifully illustrated, some with both text and speech bubbles.

In advance of a lecture I was giving in Portugal (for a former student of mine) the teachers who were to attend were invited to read a Portuguese version of *When the Moon Winked* to some children. The children were then encouraged to write their own version in Portuguese. Many captured much of the original language. One child was so close to the original that when his version was translated back into English, it closely resembled the author's version. Another child, only eight years of age, produced a fascinating illustration for this same story. He shows his grasp not only of the theme, but also of astronomy (see figure 4). Another child in Birmingham, for whom English was a second language, in a class that had access to the audio tapes, chose to retell the story with illustrations (figure 6). Like many of the other children in that class, the theme of the story was captured successfully.

Figure 4 An illustration by an 8-year-old inspired by When the Moon Winked

Figure 5 Two illustrations for class books of retold stories, by children with limited reading competence

Figure 6 A young child's book based on When the Moon Winked

Figures 7 and 8 are from *One Up* by Tony Ross, where cartoon-like illustrations were shown on screen and in the book. It is possible from the first version to grasp the theme of the story. The other examples illustrate the wide range of ability within a single class of children aged seven years of age. There was yet another example by a child in the same class, where only the odd C was recognisable, while there are attempts by five-year-olds to tell and illustrate the same story (see pages 146 and 161 in *Young Literacy Learners*). Thus, when the material is sufficiently stimulating it does enable the teacher to appreciate the gulf between the more advanced children and those with only a limited idea of written language, all within the same class.

In one class with whom I was working, after seeing the attempts of some of the children to write one of the stories I discouraged then from writing further stories for me, giving my reasons. I explained that I would not be able to guess what they meant in order to type their story for them at home. According to their teacher this proved a real incentive to them to improve. In the meantime they provided front covers and illustrations for the class books. Two examples are shown in figure 5; the first is from *Tortoise`s Tug-of-War* by Hiawyn Oram, and the second is from *Just You Wait* by Hazel Townson. See figure 9 for a story on this latter theme, stimulated by the same story, and written by a six and a half year old girl whose understanding of printed language was already much more highly developed.

I got a new tooth said Charle So
what said Tess Ive got two more
teeth than any body in the world
I bet you haven't said Charle
count them Said Tess but charle
could only count up to four charlee
changed the subject Ive got new
red boots so what Said Tess Ive
got silver ones Speicely made
for me because Ive got 12 toes
So Charle changed the subject
Ive got a dog as big as dragon
and he growls like a lion
Ive got ten monkegs they Sleep
in my bed yoar dogs not
comfey under your bed
your monkegs are toy monkey there not
Said Tess they were real Pyjamers
Two Pink Two yellow and Purple
and green. So charle changed the
Subject Ime going to the Circas
tommorow So what said Tess Ive been
twice On mon day once on Tuesday
and Im going on satueday
after nooo charle said to his
mother I don't Want Play with
Tess tomorow I want to lern
over four

Figure 7 A 7-year-old`s version of One Up

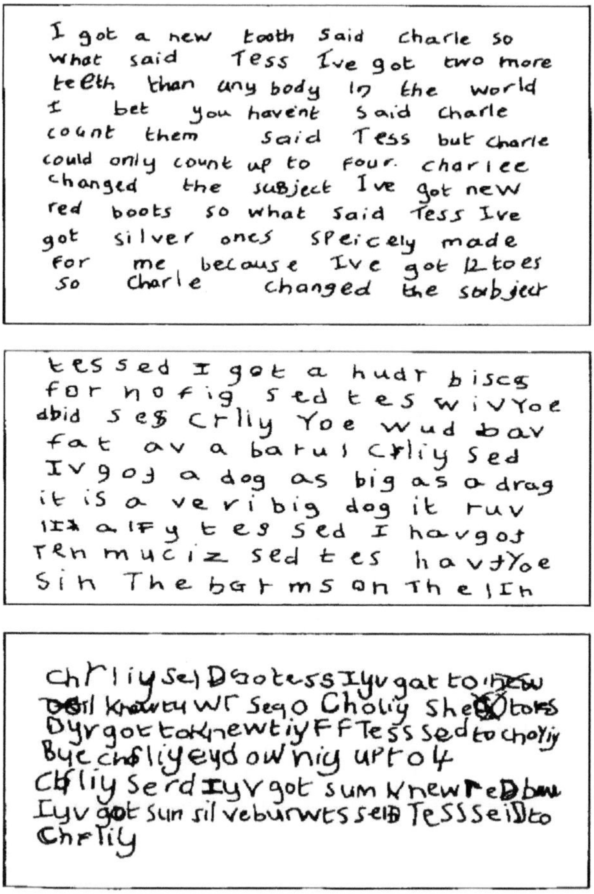

I got a new tooth said Charle so
what said Tess Ive got two more
teeth than any body in the world
I bet you havent said Charle
count them said Tess but Charle
could only count up to four. Charlee
changed the subject Ive got new
red boots so what said Tess Ive
got silver ones speicely made
for me because Ive got 12 toes
so Charle changed the subject

tessed I got a hudr biscs
for no fig sed tes wivyoe
dbid seg crliy Yoe wud bav
fat av a barus Crliy sed
Iv goj a dog as big as a drag
it is a veri big dog it ruv
ira a lfy tes sed I havgoj
Ten muciz sed tes havdYoe
Sih The barms on The lIh

Chrliy seJ Dgo tess Iyv gat to new
Deil knawty wr segqo Choliy She Otors
Dyr got toknewtiy F F Tess sed to choliy
Byc chsliy eyd own niy up to 4
Chliy serd Iyv got sum knew red bau
Iyv got sum silveburwts seb Tess sei Jto
Chrliy

Figure 8 Seven-year-olds` versions of One Up

Stimulation to tell a different story

Just You Wait by Hazel Townson stimulated a young girl to write her own story (see Figure 9). The original story on which she based it was about two brothers, Brian and Robert. In this new version there are two girls Sally and Priscilla. Another girl in a class where I was working also wrote her own version; this I typed for her with only the spelling corrected, with the heading `retold by (then her name)`. For this child also English was a second language. The full typed version is in Clark, 1994: 148. The promise of a typed version was used as a stimulus to help the children understand the function of speech marks, needed in most stories, and to encourage correct spelling.

Sally and Priscila.

One day Sally had a nice bouquet and priscila wanted it but Sally said you shall have to wait util you are bigger. The next day sally had a letter to go to the farm at 2pm in the afternoon when priscila came in for tea she saw the letter on the shelf she went to get the letter off the shelf and she road the letter and she went to see Sally I want to go to the farm too be with you said priscila but Sally said No you can not come you might fall in the mud and cut yourself. you will have to wait. On priscila's birthday she had a rocking chair that was little Sally saw her rocking chair and Said I would like that

Sally had a bouquet

a letter from the farm

But priscila sad No you will have to wait until I am bigger and then I will have a bigger chair.

priscila in her rocking chair

Figure 9 A story written at her own request by a girl aged 6 years 6 months after hearing *Just You Wait* read only once

The following story was stimulated by *King of all the Birds* by Tony Ross, which challenged one child to write a story about `Queen of all the Reptiles` with appropriate adaptation of the language as may be seen below, with the spelling and punctuation as in the original.

> It was not a happy day for the reptiles because the big ones like the alligotars, the big snakes and the dinosaurs were fighting the little ones like the lizards and turtles. They decided to have a competition to find a Queen. The reptile who could swim for the longest time would be Qeen So they started to swim lots of reptiles had a rest and only the crocodile was left "I`VE WON! She said – and a little snake came slithering out of her mouth and said "Not so fast I`m not tired and she kept on swimming and she became Queen of the reptiles.

This child was in a class that had been watching the television series. Her teacher had adopted many of the suggestions given on screen and was thus able to give a structure for the less confident, but also creative opportunities for the more advanced to make their own stories on similar themes.

Computers and literacy

Computers can be used to great effect to assist children learn the features of written English. As early as 1980s I visited a school where a programme was being used with a package that enabled the teacher to reveal as much or as little of a passage of text as he wished, certain words only, punctuation, initial letters of words, dashes for letters. The creative learning experience for these children arose from a combination of the novelty of the computer, the nature of the software and the way this teacher planned and implemented its use.

Final comments

It is hoped that the illustrations and observations in this chapter have helped to bring alive the creative possibilities of stories in developing the written language of young children. My aim was to ensure that teachers are alerted to the range of literacy development in any class of young children; that they provide creative and supportive experiences for the less advanced, and stimulation for the most advanced. The ideas I developed came from the researches I read, the researchers and creative teachers with whom I worked, and not least the children themselves who frequently surprised me with their creativity.

At the end of chapter 8 I referred to the subtleties in written English, and fun, that could be explored with young children, and in particular, the possibilities within books such as Lewis Carroll's *Alice in Wonderland* (1865) and *Through the Looking-Glass* (1872). There are numerous examples of play on words, such as lessons and lessens, tail and tale, ground flour (ground and flower).

There is space here for a few more examples:

Then you should say what you mean`, the March Hare went on.

`I do`, Alice replied, `at least I mean what I say – that`s the same thing you know`. `Not the same thing a bit`, said the Hatter.

`I see nobody on the road`, said Alice. `I wish I had such eyes`, the King remarked in a fretful tone, `to be able to see Nobody! And at that distance!`

`I think I should understand that better`, Alice said politely, `if I had it written down`, but I can`t quite follow it as you say it out loud!`

Once or twice she had peeped into the book her sister was reading, but it had no pictures or conversation in it, `and what is the use of a book`, thought Alice, `without pictures or conversation?`

Section III

Curriculum Developments and Literacy Policies, 1988 to 1997: a comparison between England and Scotland

There are two chapters in this section. In chapter 11 the developments in England and Wales, leading up to and following The Education Reform Act in 1988, are traced. English was one of the Core subjects, in which numerous modifications were made to assessment and the curriculum in the years 1988 to 1995. In 1995 I published, *Language, Learning and the Urban Child* in which I considered these developments and their effects on practice. The discussion on England and Wales is taken from that publication for which I hold the copyright.

In Scotland over that period there was no National Curriculum. A series of National Guidelines were published based on the recommendations of working parties for the age range 5-14. In a paper I delivered at a UKRA conference in 1991, `Reading in 1990s: a spring forward or a fall back?` I contrasted the developments in Scotland with those in England and Wales. This was published in 1992 in *Literacy without Frontiers*, F. Satow and B. Gatherer (eds). Subsequently I was joint editor of *Education in Scotland: policy and practice from pre-school to secondary*, M. M. Clark and P. Munn 1997 and author of three chapters, 1, 3 and 7. In chapter 1 the background to education in Scotland was described, a system very different from that in England and Wales, even in 1980s and 1990s before devolution in 1997 and the restitution of a Scottish parliament in Edinburgh. In chapter 7, `The teaching profession: its qualifications and status` was outlined. From as early as 1965 members of the teaching profession in Scotland were required to register with the General Teaching Council. The Council has played an important role in Scottish education not only with regard to discipline, but also the qualifications required of teachers; there is no comparable body in England. I have based chapter 12 in this book on chapter 3 from that publication, entitled: `Developments in primary education in Scotland`. I hold the copyright for my chapters in that book.

There are many lessons from these developments of relevance to the new National Curricula being implemented in both countries. In England during the years 1988-1997, a crucial aspect was the way in which the curriculum was driven by national assessment, not by the professionals. In Scotland, the new curriculum, A Curriculum for Excellence, has had teething problems, possibly from lack of preparation, lack of staffing or lack of funds. It is yet to be seen whether there may be more fundamental problems.

Chapter 11

The First National Curriculum in England and Wales: lessons for the future

This chapter is an edited extract from *Language Learning and the Urban Child* (Clark 1995).

The National Curriculum in England and Wales

The background

Statements that standards in our schools are falling are nothing new; often made in the absence of hard evidence. The media and politicians delight in attributing such failures to our schools, to teachers or to their trainers. Frequently cited as a cause has been some change in teaching methods it is believed has swept through the schools. Accompanying such claims is often either a call for 'back to the basics', or a return to so-called traditional methods of teaching. Claims that teachers should be trained mainly within classrooms, rather than by so-called experts, were already current in 1990s. The first extensive observational study in primary classrooms did not find evidence to support these views and still has relevance today, *Inside the Primary Classroom* (Galton, Simon and Croll, 1980):

> First, the weight of evidence on the curriculum shows very clearly that, in spite of widespread claims in the mass media, by industrialists, and by Black Paper propagandists, the general pattern of the traditional curriculum quite certainly still prevails, and has not changed in any fundamental way, let alone vanished. Such claims appear to be founded on mythology. (155)

In reports based on school inspections concern was expressed, but more often about failure in the junior school and beyond to build upon the foundations of literacy established in the early years (DES, 1991). Each successive older generation compares contemporary education unfavourably with that during their school days; they feel ill at ease if the changes are

107

dramatic. Politicians may capitalise on such beliefs, or at least find it necessary to take action to quieten the discontent. One solution has been to establish a working party! The Bullock Committee was set up because of a claimed fall in reading standards. By the time the report, *A Language for Life* (DES, 1975) was published, enthusiasm for action had waned. The Secretary of State showed no commitment to implement its far-reaching recommendations, for which he claimed no money was available.

A further working party on reading, a common focus for popular disquiet, published *The Kingman Report* (DES 1988a). This, which repeated a number of the recommendations of the Bullock Committee, was less well received by politicians than its predecessor. Its publication was followed by a further working party charged with the task of translating its recommendations into practice as a Core subject within the recently established National Curriculum in England. The chairman selected for this next working party had been one of the contributors to The Black Papers, Brian Cox. However, the recommendations of his committee met with no more general acceptance from politicians. His concern at the extent of political interference in this area is well documented by Cox himself, chosen though he was for his apparently respectable views (See *Cox on Cox*, Cox, 1991). Already by 1995 we had revisions to the recommendations made by the Cox committee, the more sensitive aspects concerning Standard English, grammar and spelling. To this was added a discussion paper on Standard English issued by SCAA (SCAA 1995a).

Numerous other reports could be cited, some from select committees of the House of Commons, others from working parties. They made valuable recommendations that proved too expensive to be implemented, did not meet with political approval, or were overtaken by other changes. Two only will be mentioned here, both though not specifically within the remit of the National Curriculum, were affected by its implementation. The Warnock Committee on *Special Educational Needs*, was the first committee of enquiry specifically charged to review educational provision for all handicapped children. *Special Educational Needs* (HMSO 1978) recommended that:

The planning of services for children and young people should be based on the assumption that about one in six children at any time and up to one in five children at some time during their school career will require some form of special educational provision. (338)

Legislation was set in train to assist the implementation of the recommendations. However, the developments following the Education Reform Act of 1988, in particular the proposal to publish league tables ranking schools on the basis of their pupils' performance on the national assessment at each key stage, inevitably led to teachers being less willing to accept children whose special educational needs could only be met at the expense of other children in their class, or who might adversely affect the schools' standing on the league tables. A so-called market economy in schools is not conducive to provision for children with special needs within mainstream education.

An all-party Select Committee of the House of Commons report, *Educational Provision for the Under Fives* (House of Commons, 1989) was followed by a debate in the House of Commons. The outcome was that the Secretary of State announced yet another committee, charged with drawing up a curriculum for children under five, to be chaired by an Education Minister, Angela Rumbold. The disturbing feature was not only that it appeared to be an attempt to appease those who were not happy with the recommendations of the Select Committee, but also that it was chaired by a nominated politician, who also selected the members for this committee concerned with devising a curriculum, to include 'among others' experts in education! *Starting with Quality* (HMSO 1990), the report of the Rumbold Committee, did reinforce some of the recommendations made elsewhere, and was referred to in the draft proposals for the curriculum for preschool education. Since then, political interference in determining the content of the curriculum in a number of subject areas has continued to be apparent within the National Curriculum.

The development of the National Curriculum

The National Curriculum for England and Wales with Core and other Foundation subjects and national assessment at the end of key stages was introduced in the Education Reform Act of 1988. In the same year The National Curriculum Council was set up to establish and review the curriculum for all state schools, with a parallel body in Wales. Duncan Graham, was chairman and chief executive of NCC during the formative years from 1988 until 1991. A *Lesson for Us All* (Graham and Tytler 1993), painted a disturbing picture of the way that the developments in the various subjects were manipulated by a succession of Secretaries of State. History is one example cited, in that decisions about history were, `the result of a Dutch auction between Clarke and his officials` (60-70). Graham believed, as did many others, that the time was ripe for some form of national curriculum to ensure a higher standard in education, with breadth and a reduction in the massive inequalities in standards between the best and the poorest of our schools. However, he felt that it was crucial that there should be an independent body with the power to monitor and evaluate the curriculum after its introduction into schools, `to ensure that any change is soundly based and not subject to political whim or prejudice` (95). From his description it is clear why the curriculum for the various core and other foundation subjects proved to be unmanageable and lacking in co-ordination across subjects. Little consultation took place between the various working parties, each of which regarded its subject as the most important. It is thus no surprise that radical revisions, and a drastic slimming down should have proved essential, along the lines recommended in the report of the enquiry by Sir Ron Dearing commissioned by the Secretary of State for Education. (Dearing, 1994)

A crucial element in the National Curriculum was the assessment at the end of each Key Stage, the planning for which was the responsibility of the School Examinations and Assessment Council. The rationale for the assessment was laid out in the report of the Task Group on Assessment and Testing. (TGAT) (DES 1988b) Paul Black who chaired that committee lamented the failure to put into practice its recommendations. (Black 1994) He claimed there is ample evidence that prior to 1988, `assessment as an

110

integral part of a teaching programme was a concept that was hardly understood at all by the majority of teachers`, yet unfortunately `the introduction of national assessment has made very little difference to this situation`. (130) One major problem with assessment within the National Curriculum was that there was an increasing focus on assessment by externally devised national Standard Assessment Tests (SATs). Improvement of assessment by teachers as an integral part of their teaching was not given the important role envisaged in the TGAT recommendations. Black and others would argue that priority was given by politicians and those in powerful positions to summative assessment devised to compare standards between schools, with accountability as the focus. This was at the expense of the valuable but much more complex formative assessment. In *National Curriculum Assessment: A review of policy 1987-1994,* Daugherty (1995) expressed concern at the way the plans for assessment had developed; this from someone who was for three years a member of the School Examinations and Assessment Council, and later Chairman of the Curriculum Council for Wales. He stated that:

> in practice, there is no better way of ensuring that assessment drives the curriculum in inappropriate ways than to leave the determination of assessment methods and procedures until after the curriculum itself is finalized. (183)

He further pointed out that `only two of the fifteen members of the original School Examinations and Assessment Council, appointed by ministers actually worked in schools`. (167-8) He remained critical of the plans for assessment even post-Dearing.

English in the National Curriculum

English remains a high profile subject politically, one where there were frequent changes made to the content of the curriculum and assessment. The extent of the inclusion of phonics teaching in the early stages of teaching reading, the importance of Standard English, of spelling and punctuation, were of concern at the primary school stage; in secondary schools, the choice of prescribed reading. The amount of paper on this one subject circulated in information to schools was enormous. NB These comments are from my 1995 paper! The pressures on the teaching of English placed on schools in England and Wales came not only from the introduction of The National Curriculum in English as one of the Core Subjects, and its first national assessment when the children were barely seven years of age. Other problems were: the numerous changes made and the greater emphasis on SATs rather than teacher assessment. The inclusion of assessment of mathematics and science for seven-year-olds left teachers with less time to spend on English, because of their insecurity in the other areas. Comparison of schools' performance by league tables based on SATs, was without any allowance for the very different starting points of the children, and in some schools the large numbers of children for whom English was a second language. Research projects funded to analyse the effects of the changes were barely completed, or their results widely accessible, before revisions to the curriculum as well as its assessment were introduced, some seemed to owe much to political pressures.

By April 1993, *English for ages 5-16* (DFE 1993), had been issued, which it was claimed: emphasised the importance of Standard English; a more precise definition of the skills involved in learning to read; more explicit information on how pupils should be introduced to 'great literature'; defined more precisely the basic writing skills and grammatical knowledge which pupils need to master; ways in which competence in spelling can be developed. Sir Ron Dearing was then charged with the task of reviewing the whole National Curriculum. By 1994, new draft proposals for English had appeared.

The continual tinkering with the English curriculum over a period of seven years and the assessment procedures, made it confusing for teachers to tease out the key recommendations, even to become familiar with the testing procedures. Teachers' concern at the extra work made it necessary to introduce external marking. Thus, it was unlikely the assessment would lead to insights into the needs of the children as only global scores would be available.

By 1990s there was a more sensitive approach to the introduction of Standard English, full stops, correct spelling and correct letter orientation and accuracy in oral reading, than seemed destined to appear. What seems to be lacking was an emphasis on the purposes of communication, on how to translate our knowledge of the way children learn to be literate into classroom practice. In, *English: A review of inspection findings 1993-94* (OFSTED 1995), it was stated that across all key stages standards of achievement in English were satisfactory or better in four-fifths of schools. Concern was expressed at the relatively poorer performance of boys; at a lack of book resources in a significant minority of schools; and that pupils of higher ability tended to experience better teaching than those of low ability. At Key Stage 2 too great use of decontextualised and undemanding exercises was criticised. Following the revisions and slimming down of the National Curriculum recommended by Dearing (1994), he proposed that there should be a pause on curriculum reform for five years.

An evaluation of the curriculum

The curriculum in schools in England probably became more balanced and with greater breadth for more pupils than was the case before the Education Reform Act of 1988. A necessary structure of accountability was being built into each stage of the system. It was hoped that:

> any relative success of the curriculum is not offset by political interventions in methodology, based on the belief that it is possible to return to a fondly remembered and often illusory golden age. (Graham and Tytler, 1993: 119)

One must question whether the years between 1988 and 1995 led to greater equality for those with greatest need. This includes those in deprived inner-city areas; children whose mother tongue is other than English; whose culture is very different from that of the majority and children with special educational needs.

The report *Access and Achievement in Urban Education* (OFSTED 1993), summarises evidence from a survey conducted in 1991 in seven urban areas of England characterised by high levels of social and economic disadvantage. It is claimed that:

> The residents of disadvantaged urban areas covered by this survey are poorly served by the education system. Weaknesses of provision within individual institutions are exacerbated by poor links between them. (6)

In *Education in England 1990-91* (HMI 1992) concern was expressed at the less satisfactory standards of work in schools serving areas of marked social and economic disadvantage. Good standards of work were found in some schools in all areas. In such schools there was:

> effective leadership; teaching of a consistently high quality; carefully planned, well-managed classwork; a low turnover of staff; and good teaching resources. (9)

Similar concerns were expressed in a report by The House of Commons Education Committee (1995), where the importance of purposeful and effective leadership in schools is stressed; of finding ways to encourage able, experienced teachers to work in city schools and remain there long enough to provide stability and continuity; of sharing best practice among schools. It is disturbing to note that in the debates surrounding the Education Reform Bill, and subsequently there was little evidence of an awareness of the needs of children whose language and culture is not that of the majority. Furthermore, only recently has concern been expressed at possible problems for children in rural areas.

We cannot yet be sure the extent to which the large inequalities in access to the curriculum are being eroded, and whether teacher expectations of their pupils are being raised where these were previously found to be low. Researches and HMI inspections showed just how wide the gulf was between the best and the poorest schools. Only some of these are factors beyond the control of the school, evidenced by the fact that both the curriculum and standards differed widely in schools with similar intakes (Tizard *et al*, 1988). There are lessons to be learnt from a study of schools that made demonstrable improvements (see *Improving Schools,* OFSTED 1994).

In *Learning to Succeed* (National Commission on Education 1993), concern was expressed at a number of the developments in education being imposed on schools, in particular the publication of league tables at Key Stage 1, revealing as they do more about the school's intake than the primary schools themselves. The need to raise expectations; to develop pupils' thinking skills; to support their independent learning; to foster their creativity are all given high priority in that report. The importance of the new technologies is stressed and their potential for improving learning and the value of using the resources in the community beyond the school. Sadly there has been little evidence that this wide ranging important report had any major influence on government planning. (See the follow-up report, *Learning to Succeed: the way ahead,* The National Commission on Education, 1995).

Assessment and the National Curriculum

SATs and assessment

By the time of the General Election in 1992 the Secretary of State for Education already had access to the findings of a report of research commissioned by the Government that confirmed the relationship between a number of background variables and performance on the SATs of seven-year-olds at the end of Key Stage 1. He still insisted on publishing league tables of results by individual school and by local authority as a measure of school performance uncorrected for any background features. Some months later, and without publicity the results of the ENCA 1 Project were released (see Graham and Tytler, 1993: 127-8). The following are among the findings:

girls' scores were significantly better than boys in English;

there were significant differences in SATS scores on all subjects between children of different ages at the time of SATs when tested (the age range was from 7 years 8 months to 6 years 9 months at the time of testing, a very wide spread);

- there were significant differences in performance between ethnic groups;
- the performance of children whose first language was not English was significantly lower;
- there was a declining pattern of attainment for children from high status neighbourhoods to low status.

(From *The Evaluation of National Curriculum Assessment at Key Stage 1*, Shorrocks, 1992).

The Government accepted the recommendations in the Dearing report that assessment at the end of Key Stage 1 should be slimmed down, and that only the national aggregate results of the assessment of 7 and 14 year olds should be published, not school by school in performance tables (Dearing 1994). The report also stressed the importance of investigating an approach to the assessment of 'the value-added' by individual schools. The School Curriculum and Assessment Authority noted that the national test results for 1994 showed that even by the end of Key Stage 1 girls were out performing boys. This was still true for English in Key Stage 3 results (SCAA, 1995b). Even this crude measure has implications when judging the relative performance of single sex schools, or schools where the majority of pupils are boys. Without information from Baseline Assessment any attempt to use results at the end of Key Stage 1 to hold schools accountable does injustice to those facing the greatest challenge. However, there are dangers that in baseline assessments some young children will be seriously underestimated. There is a massive literature on the dangers of assuming reliability of any assessment of young children, even from standardised tests; such assessments require well trained assessors. The results are influenced by the children's willingness to respond to questioning, the length of their answers and their willingness to risk-take when they are not sure. In general, the more experience a young child has of relating to a number of different adults the more likely is any assessment to be reliable.

Teacher assessment

As indicated earlier, the emphasis in the national assessment was predominantly on summative not formative assessment, on accountability. The Government did come to accept that teacher assessment should have equal weight with test results in reporting to parents. We need to ensure that teachers appreciate the importance of diagnostic assessment, and that they are helped to become more sophisticated in monitoring children's progress. In Reports on Pupils` Achievements in 1994/95 (DFE Circular 1/95) the requirements for reports to parents of their children's progress are listed. One must wonder how meaningful to many parents were the types of reports recommended in the circular and how its contents could have been made more helpful. Continuity between primary and secondary schools was not given high priority in England and Wales within the National Curriculum; each phase was concerned with the massive changes in curriculum and assessment within its own phase.

Raising reading standards

That literacy is a crucial element in any attempt to raise standards of education was recognised, with the designation of 1995 as 'The Year of Reading' in England. Many new initiatives were underway, with schools encouraged to bid for additional funds for development projects. Birmingham was one of the LEAs to receive government support for a pilot scheme to develop Reading Recovery over three years. The cost effectiveness of Reading Recovery in a two year evaluation by the Thomas Coram Unit was reported in *Early Intervention in Children with Reading Difficulties: An evaluation of reading recovery and a phonological training* (SCAA, 1995c). The report by The House of Commons Education Committee, *Performance in City Schools* (1995) recommended that DfE should continue funding Reading Recovery, and that a range of programmes aimed to improve literacy should be funded and monitored to identify the advantages and disadvantages of each. The following were recommended:

- partnership with parents;

- support in the classroom from peers and older children, from parents and other volunteers hearing reading;
- awareness of the value of helping children to appreciate the relationship between reading and writing from the earliest stages;
- libraries and librarians to be recognised as an important resource to schools and for individual children.

I felt that insufficient attention in the funded projects on reading was paid to encouraging children to read for information, helping them to develop effective strategies for doing so and to the role of computers in the development of literacy.

In a presentation to a meeting of The Society of Authors on electronic publishing Chris Barlas made a number of pertinent observations:

> I cannot imagine that this new technology will suddenly expunge all human culture from the face of the earth and present us with something totally new. It is only technology. It is only fear and ignorance that will hold us back from picking up these new pens. (Barlas 1995: 7)

The way ahead

In *Education Divides: Poverty and schooling in the 1990s* (Smith and Noble, 1995), the authors claim that recent reforms had increased the gulf between the more and less advantaged. They point out that in international comparisons where we score poorly in the United Kingdom, the prime reason lies not in performance at the top of the range, but in a long tail of low performance. They list the following as some of the features known to have lasting effects for children from poor families: high quality preschool provision; special reading schemes such as Reading Recovery; reductions in class size for young children; more effective schools and parental involvement.

Did the National Curriculum of 1988 and its modifications in England and Wales indeed improve the opportunities for learning we offer in our schools? Were the subject areas too rigidly defined in watertight compartments, or too fragmented to provide children with opportunities to develop their understanding, to integrate their knowledge and stimulate their creativity? What effect did the types of national attainment measures have on the curriculum and on the expectations of parents and teachers? Were the assessments, their content, timing or even the way the results were reported, the most powerful influence on what subjects were taught, on the subject content and what was given high priority?

In Scotland was the approach any more successful in improving the literacy context in primary and secondary schools? This will be considered in the following chapter. The issues discussed in this chapter remain of relevance as England introduces a new curriculum. Have we learnt any lessons?

References

Barlas, C. (1995) `Voices in Cyberspace`. Paper presented at a meeting of the Society of Authors: London (unpublished).

Black, P. (1994) `Alternative education policies: assessment and testing`. In S. Tomlinson, (ed.) *Educational Reform and its Consequences*. London: IPPR/Rivers Oram.

Cox, B. (1991) *Cox on Cox: an English Curriculum for the 1990s.* London: Hodder and Stoughton.

Daugherty, R. (1995) *National Curriculum Assessment: a review of policy 1987-1994.* London: Falmer Press.

Dearing, R. (1994) *The National Curriculum and its Assessment.* London: SCAA.

DES (1975) *A Language for Life.* (The Bullock Report). London. HMSO.

DES (1988a) *Report of the Enquiry into the Teaching of English Language.* (The Kingman Report). London: HMSO.

DES (1988b) *National Curriculum: Task group on assessment and testing: A report.* London: DES and Welsh Office.

DES (1991) *The Teaching and Learning of Reading in Primary Schools.* A report by HMI. London: DES.

DFE (1993) *English for ages 5-15.* London: DFE.

DFE (1995) *Report on Pupils' Achievements in 1994/95.* Circular 1/95. London: DFE.

Galton, M., Simon, B. and Croll, P. (1980) *Inside the Primary Classroom.* London: Routledge and Kegan Paul.

Graham, D. and Tytler, D. (1993) *A Lesson For Us All: the making of the national curriculum.* London: Routledge.

HMI (1992) *Education in England 1990-91.* The Annual Report of HM Senior Chief Inspector of Schools. London: DES.

HMSO (1978) *Special Educational Needs.* (The Warnock Report) London: HMSO.

HMSO (1990) *Starting with Quality.* (The Rumbold Report). London: HMSO.

House of Commons (1989) *Educational Provision for the Under Fives.* Education Science and Arts Committee London: HMSO.

House of Commons (1995) *Performance in City Schools.* Education Committee. London: HMSO.

National Commission on Education (1993) *Learning to Succeed: a radical look at education today and a strategy for the future.* London; Heinemann.

National Commission on Education (1995) *Learning to Succeed: the way ahead*. London: The National Commission.

OFSTED (1993) *Access and Achievement in Urban Education*. London: HMSO.

OFSTED (1994) *Improving Schools*. London: HMSO.

OFSTED (1995) *English: a review of inspection findings 1993-94*. London: HMSO.

SCAA (1995a) *Children's Use of Spoken Standard English*. SCAA Discussion Papers No. 1. London: SCAA.

SCAA (1995b) *Consistency in Teacher Assessment: Guidance for schools: Key Stages 1 to 3*. London: SCAA.

SCAA (1995c) *Early Intervention in Children with Reading Difficulties: an evaluation of Reading Recovery and a phonological training*. SCAA Discussion Papers: No. 2 London: SCAA.

Shorrocks, D. (1992) *The Evaluation of National Curriculum Assessment at Key Stage 1 (ENCA 1 Project)*. Leeds: School of Education, University of Leeds.

Smith, T. and Noble, M. (1995) *Education Divides: poverty and schooling in the 1990s*. London: CPAG.

Tizard, B., Blatchford, P., Burke, J., Farquhar, C. and Plewis, I. (1988) *Young Children at School in the Inner City*. Hove: Lawrence Erlbaum.

NB *Education in England: a brief history*, Gilliard, D. 2011, available online, is a valuable resource, with links to official reports and education acts. www.educationengland.org.uk/history

Chapter 12

Government Policy on Literacy in Scotland from 1980s to 1990s

This chapter is based on chapters 1 and 3 in *Education in Scotland: policy and practice from pre-school to secondary*, M. M. Clark and P. Munn. (eds). London: Routledge. 1997.

The background to The National Guidelines

Setting the scene

The impression is often given that the curriculum and assessment in Scotland is similar to that elsewhere in the United Kingdom. However, the organisation of and developments in education in Scotland differed fundamentally from those in England, even before devolution in 1997. At the time of devolution, Scotland had a population of about five million, of a total population of about 58 million in the United Kingdom. The United Kingdom parliament was in London, and only a minority of its members were from Scotland. Yet, even under the Conservative government in power for the eighteen years before devolution, a government that had been described as hostile to Scottish distinctiveness, many features survived with regard to education and the legal system.

Several background features are of relevance to education in Scotland. First, Scotland is the most sparsely populated part of the United Kingdom; in 1994 more than half the primary schools in Scotland had fewer than 200 pupils. There were high levels of poverty with, in 1995, 20% of the population entitled to free school meals, with wide variation between areas. In 1994-1995, 96% of the school population were in local authority schools. At that time there were no statistics from the Scottish Office for those whose mother tongue was not English or those from ethnic minorities. However, from the census in 1991 it is clear that the situation was very different from that in England. In England, 6.4% of the population were from ethnic minorities; in Scotland it was 1.3%, with the majority of these of Pakistani or Indian origin, and the second largest group Chinese. In Scotland at the time of the census in 1991, 1.4% of the population over three years of age spoke, read or wrote Gaelic.

Education in Scotland remained organised separately from that in the rest of the United Kingdom following the Union in 1707, and there were separate acts of parliament governing most aspects of Scottish education, although these had to be passed by parliament in London. While the Secretary of State for Education was responsible for education in England, the Scottish Education Department, based in Edinburgh, had a ministerial team headed by the Secretary of State for Scotland, who was a member of Cabinet. Ofsted, the inspection body in England had no responsibility in Scotland, where the body responsible was Her Majesty's Inspectorate. From 1965 there was a General Teaching Council in Scotland with which teachers were required to register. (see Clark in Clark and Munn. 1997: chapter 7)

The curriculum and assessment in Scottish schools

The developments in the curriculum and assessment during the years 1988 to 1997 increased rather than reduced differences between education in Scotland and that in England and Wales. The Scottish Consultative Council on the Curriculum (SCCC) was the principal advisory body to the Secretary of State for Scotland on all matters relating to the curriculum for 3 to 18-year-olds. It kept the Scottish school curriculum under review; issued guidance on the curriculum and carried out programmes of curriculum development, consulting with interested groups and individuals. Its publication, *Teaching for Effective Learning,* the subject of widespread consultation, apparently met with an enthusiastic response (SCCC, 1996).

There was no national curriculum in Scotland in the years 1988 to 1997, unlike in England and Wales. The National Guidelines for the age range 5-14 were developed between 1987 and 1993, based on reports from working parties of professionals closely involved in work in schools. The reason for the focus on 5-14 was that there were already developments underway in the curriculum for children aged 14+. Unlike the National Curriculum in England, the guidelines did not represent a sharp change from previous policy. They laid emphasis on balance, breadth and continuity in children's learning. An outline of the programme was to be found in *The Structure and Balance of the Curriculum 5-14* (SOED, 1993). The target was for all guidelines to be implemented by 1998-1999. Assessment and reporting formed an integral part of the programme, with emphasis on teacher assessment, and materials for diagnostic assessment in English, mathematics and science. Furthermore, the recommendations of the working parties were adopted as national guidelines with only minor alterations. There were neither repeated changes, nor was there the political interference with the curriculum as in England and Wales during these years (see chapter 11). Teachers, advisers and college lecturers played an important part in planning the curriculum and related assessment in Scotland. The working parties and guidelines all covered the full age range 5-14 and stressed the need for balance, breadth and continuity in children's learning, both within the primary school, and between primary and secondary school.

In Scotland there was also a programme of testing, but there were no league tables based on national testing. There was no compulsory testing of children at either seven or eleven years of age, as in England at that time. The structure reflected recognition of the teacher as a professional who should make continuous assessment of a pupil's progress.

Subject groupings under the National Guidelines
No education act was passed to determine the changes. Two existing committees were charged with planning the developments. The subjects were grouped in five areas, namely, English, mathematics, environmental studies (including social subjects, science and health and technology subjects), expressive arts (art and design, drama, music and physical education) and religious and moral education. There were also guidelines on Assessment 5-14 and The Structure and Balance of the Curriculum 5-14.

The National Guidelines for English

National Guidelines for English in Scotland were very similar to the recommendations of that working party and gave much greater recognition to the diversity of culture and language within the community than was apparent in the reports in England. The Scottish guidelines for English, showed a desire to foster respect for this in young children throughout their school career. To quote:

> Young Scots, many of them bilingual, are growing up in a culturally diverse society, in an increasingly interdependent world. Schools should therefore create an ethos and generate a curriculum which will recognise languages other than English and lead pupils to enjoy and benefit from the varied languages and cultures in the community....All pupils can increase their respect for and understanding of other cultures by reading literature which gives insights into the values of Non-European cultures, and the ways of life of the varied communities of modern Britain. (SOED, 1991: 59)

National tests were required in only English and mathematics, and were initially introduced only for children who had completed three years in primary school, that is about eight years of age, and those at the end of their primary schooling. National tests were to be a back-up to teacher assessment and were to be administered when the teacher's assessment indicated that the pupil had achieved the attainment at a particular level, not in a particular year in the primary school. English tests involved two tests of silent reading for comprehension, one of a narrative passage, and one for information. There were two assessments of writing, with children expected to write on a narrative and information topic. Their writing was assessed for choice and use of language, selection and organisation of ideas and technical skills. The teachers chose the tests from a catalogue on topics to suit their children's interests from a large bank of such materials.

The developments in Scotland in contrast to England

A number of important features in the planning of the curricular proposals in Scotland differed from those in England over the years 1988-1997:

1. Existing committees were charged with making the recommendations for the curriculum and assessment, not new committees as in England.

2. The membership of the working parties set up by the Scottish Consultative Council on the Curriculum reflected the wide range of professionals involved in schools, teachers in primary schools and subject specialists in secondary schools, head teachers from different sizes of school, advisers and directors of education, college lecturers and professionals on secondment to SCCC. On the working parties was someone with expertise in the education of children with special needs, thus attention was paid to the needs of such children.

3. A general framework was common to all the working papers and guidelines; all covered the age range 5-14. These included recommendations for attainment outcomes and targets for programmes of study.

4. The guidelines, which were published after a period of consultation, appear to retain the main recommendations of the working parties.

5. In Scotland, following the publications of the guidelines, the schools were encouraged to implement the proposals, with the aim of full implementation by 1998-1999, without as in England over that period amendments and revisions.

6. Working party reports on assessment and reporting, with a focus on improving classroom assessment and partnership with parents, were being issued for consultation at the same time as the curriculum documents.

7. The general statement from the Scottish Office on the under-fives curriculum was based largely on HMI visits to a number of under-five units (SOED, 1994). It reiterated the importance of play and emphasised the importance of cultivating children's natural learning processes through a carefully planned curriculum in every kind of pre-school unit (see Watt in Clark and Munn 1997: chapter 2). There was a link with the 5-14 programme with an emphasis on literacy and numeracy as well as emotional, personal, creative and

physical skills, to contribute to children's knowledge and understanding of the world (SOED, 1994).

The way ahead

Following the reestablishment of a Scottish Parliament in Edinburgh in 1999, education in Scotland became the responsibility of the Scottish Parliament. Scotland has already embarked on its new curriculum in 2010, A Curriculum for Excellence, with the aim of providing a coherent and enriched curriculum for the age range 3-18. What lessons, if any have we learnt?

References

Clark, M. M. and Munn, P. (eds) (1997) *Education in Scotland: policy and practice from pre-school to secondary.* London: Routledge.

SCCC (1996) *Teaching for Effective Learning.* Dundee: SCCC.

SOED (1991) *Curriculum and Assessment in Scotland. National Guidelines: English Language 5-14.* Edinburgh: HMSO.

SOED (1993) *Curriculum and Assessment in Scotland: National Guidelines. The Structure and Balance of the Curriculum 5-14.* Edinburgh: HMSO.

SOED (1994) *The Education of Children Under 5 in Scotland.* Edinburgh: HMSO.

Section IV

Government Policy in England on Learning to Read 2006 to 2014

The origins of the Coalition Government's policy in England for the teaching of reading can be traced back to the Rose Report in 2006, which under the previous Labour Government raised the issue of synthetic phonics as the way to teaching reading. A critique of that report is to be found in chapter 13. The following five chapters in this section focus on the development of this policy under the Coalition Government between 2010 and 2014. All the chapters in this section are adapted from articles in the *Education Journal* published between 2006 and 2014.

In Chapter 13 the Rose Report on beginning reading, published in 2006, is discussed. It was commissioned following an enquiry by a Select Committee of the House of Commons, at the request of the Labour Government then in power. Its claims for synthetic phonics as the method for teaching beginning reading have had a major impact in both schools and on the training of teachers in England, the basis for the Coalition Government's policy since 2010.

In Chapter 14 there is an analysis of the evidence base for a claim that there is indeed one best method of teaching reading for all children and that synthetic phonics is that method. Not only is the research cited by the government in support of its claim discussed, but other researches ignored by the government are considered. From 2011 to October 2013 match-funding was made available for schools in England to purchase synthetic phonics materials and training courses from a recommended list, also those training teachers were instructed to make synthetic phonics the focus for their courses. In 2012 a phonics check was introduced for all children in Year 1 (aged about 6 years of age) in England. In Chapter 15 the development of the phonics check is discussed and the results of the first year of its implementation. The National Foundation for Educational Research was commissioned to undertake a three year research into the

129

effects of the check. The first report of that research is discussed in Chapter 16. In Chapter 17 an appraisal is made of the reliability and validity of the check following the second year if its administration. In Chapter 18 information is provided on some of the costs of the policy, obtained under the Freedom of Information Act. While the focus in this section has been on developments in England over the past few years the issues are of much wider significance. Some aspects of these policies are current in other countries also, with similar claims that they are based on research evidence. These include USA, France, Germany and in some developing countries. These claims are considered in the second part of chapter 18.

The powerful place of commercial interests in governments' choice of policies and the materials recommended, and even funded for the teaching of reading is one disturbing feature.

All six chapters are based on articles published in the *Education Journal,* chapter 13 in 2006, the others in 2013 and 2014. I am grateful to Demitri Coryton of Education Publishing for permission to include amended versions of the articles.

Chapter 13

The Rose Report and the Teaching of Reading: a critique

This chapter is based on an article published in the *Education Journal* (Issue 97, 2006: 27-29). As may be seen, claims for synthetic phonics as the method of teaching reading pre date the edicts from the Coalition Government in England since 2010 discussed in the following chapters.

Introduction

A summary of the Rose Report, Independent Review of the Teaching of Early Reading: final report, appeared in *Education Journal* (Issue 94 2006, 28). In the same issue, in an article by Colin Richards entitled, 'This could be the end of teacher autonomy', Professor Richards commented: 'Well in a few months time teachers of young children could be required to teach initial reading through synthetic phonics – a method not dissimilar to those used in Victorian classrooms'.

The background to the Rose Enquiry

The decision to establish this inquiry was stimulated by the report of the all-party House of Commons Education and Skills Committee, *Teaching Children to Read* (April 2005). The publicity from the media and from politicians around that report had as its main focus phonics, more particularly synthetic phonics. Much of the oral evidence presented to the Committee was from proponents of synthetic phonics, several of them with a commercial interest in programmes for schools. Rhona Johnston was questioned on evidence from her research in primary schools in Clackmannanshire, a small county in Scotland. Thereafter Clackmannanshire was frequently cited in England, though few references identified the precise nature of this research.

The Select Committee recommendations

It is worth reminding readers that the House of Commons Select Committee that led to the setting up of the Rose enquiry stressed that:

Whatever method is used in the early stages of teaching children to read, we are convinced that inspiring an enduring enjoyment of reading should be a key objective. This can be endangered both by an overtly formal approach in the early years and by a failure to teach decoding. (36)

The Committee also recommended that an inquiry should be established and evidence should be sought to establish among other points:

How long any gains from a particular programme are sustained; the effectiveness of different approaches with particular groups of children, including boys/girls, those with special educational needs and those with a high level of socio-economic disadvantage. (36)

They stressed that the research study should:

- measure and compare attainment by means of standardised testing, not Key Stage test results;
- measure attainment of all components of literacy (word recognition, reading comprehension, narrative awareness, etc.);
- use control groups to take account of factors which may have a bearing on reading outcomes, for example teacher knowledge and ability; socio-economic background; gender. (37)

No such research was funded.

Setting for the Rose Report

Following the report of the Select Committee, on 22 June 2005 the then Secretary of State for Education, Ruth Kelly, wrote to Jim Rose, who had agreed to her request to lead an independent review of best practice in the teaching of early reading and the range of strategies to best support children who have fallen behind. In her letter to Jim Rose, she set out three points she wished to be considered as follows:

- What our expectations of best practice should be in the teaching of early reading and synthetic phonics for primary schools and early years settings, including both the content and the pace of teaching.
- How this relates to the development of the birth-to-five framework and the ongoing development and renewal of the National Literacy Framework for teaching.
- What range of provision best supports children with significant literacy difficulties and enables them to catch up with their peers, and the relationship of such targeted intervention programmes with synthetic phonics teaching.

Jim Rose was asked to provide an interim report by November 2005 with his full report early in 2006. Following the interim report in December 2005 already Ruth Kelly was making it clear that she was fully in support of the report's recommendation that a systematic, direct teaching of synthetic phonics should be the first strategy taught to all children learning to read, introduced by the age of five.

The Rose Report

The Final Rose Report in March 2006 contained a wide range of recommendations designed to improve the teaching of reading. However, all the attention seems to have been focused on the synthetic phonics issue. This is not surprising in view of the statements by the Secretary of State who commissioned the report and the fact that already by page 3 the report states:

Engaging young children in interesting and worthwhile pre-reading activities paves the way for the great majority to make a good start on systematic phonic work by the age of five. Indeed, for some, an earlier start may be possible and desirable.

Among the reactions to the interim report were concerns that the recommendations could be seen as claiming that one size fits all. The Rose Report did acknowledge the research evidence that children benefit from learning the names of the letters of the alphabet as well as the sounds (26), though I have not seen reference to that in any comments.

Parents must have been concerned or confused at the mixed messages they were receiving from the media following the Rose report about their role in their children's early learning to read; this at a time when research had shown just how much parents can and do contribute.

There was a lack of reference in the report to provision for young children who are already able to read with fluency and understanding when they enter school, also those children whose language difficulties may make a focus on phonics at too early an age a stumbling block to their learning. Not all reading specialists would agree with the following:

> An early start on systematic phonic work is especially important for those children who do not have the advantages of strong support for literacy at home. (31)

Critique of the Rose Report

Many young children now entering school are already more computer-literate than their teachers in this age of digital literacy. This deserves more attention than it appears to have received in the Rose Report (see *Popular Culture, New Media and Digital Literacy in Early Childhood* J. Marsh, (ed) 2005).

Why in the United Kingdom, in England in particular, is it considered to be progress to introduce children to reading, and especially phonics, so early and so long before the teaching of reading takes place in most other countries? This includes many with higher standards of literacy than England. Surely there is a case to be made for broadening the curriculum and for delaying the teaching of reading. This might make such instruction less time-consuming as a consequence of the children's greater maturity and better-developed listening skills.

From the pronouncements of some politicians and others, the impression was given that an injection of synthetic phonics first, fast and only as soon as children enter school, will solve all reading problems. Some of the invective has been reminiscent of the hype that surrounded the introduction of ita (the initial teaching alphabet) over 40 years ago. Had synthetic phonics now taken the place of the initial teaching alphabet?

I was concerned when I became aware of this as the Government's solution to the scale of illiteracy in this country, or at least the failure in England to reach the hoped-for targets in literacy by the end of Key Stage 2 in primary school.

The Clackmannanshire Research

The Rose Committee did visit Clackmannanshire and several pages in the report are devoted to the approach to the teaching of literacy they found there, but there is no critical evaluation of the research (61-5). Therefore it is important to note that in that research, the comparison was not between phonics and no phonics, but different amounts, speeds and types of phonics programmes within an early intervention programme. Frequent reference was made in the media to the 'spectacular' results from that research, in particular the results for the boys. It should be noted that the more spectacular results were in the children's word recognition skills, rather than in their understanding. By Primary 7 (the end of primary school in Scotland) the group taught initially by synthetic phonics were cited as reading 3 years 6 months ahead of chronological age, spelling was 1 year 8 months ahead. However, reading comprehension was only 3.5 months ahead.

Criticisms of the methodology of the research have been voiced by a number of experts, some in Scotland, including lack of attention to other aspects of the programme in these primary schools. The county was involved in an early intervention study with funding from the Scottish Executive. Concerned that the hype was in danger of spreading from the

135

media in England to Scotland, as the First Minister had become `the most recent evangelist for synthetic phonics`, Sue Ellis was interviewed for a leading article in TES Scotland on 2 September 2005 (by Elizabeth Buie). She expressed concern, `that one study which has had no external validation now appears to be dictating educational policy`. She also expressed irritation that complex research is being `converted into sound bites`. In an article in TES Scotland entitled 'Phonics is just the icing on the cake', (TES Scotland 23 September 2005), Ellis pointed out that the schools in that research did not just do phonics. She undertook a careful analysis of what was entailed by the intervention in Clackmannanshire, in addition to the comparison of the two types of phonics. In brief, there was a varied programme: nursery nurses were introduced into Primary 1, story bags; home-link teachers; homework clubs and nurture groups. Furthermore the staff development programme for teachers was a rolling programme that began with Primary 1 teachers, then Primary 2 and caught teachers transferred to a new stage. The programme for teachers stressed making learning purposeful, motivating children and the importance of noticing and building on success.

The Report by Torgerson, Brooks and Hall (2006)

In parallel with the Rose inquiry, the DfES had commissioned `A Systematic Review of the Research Literature on the Use of Phonics in the Teaching of Reading and Spelling` by the Universities of York and Sheffield. This report was submitted in late 2005 and appeared in early 2006 (Torgerson *et al.* 2006). I was therefore surprised to find that it did not appear on the reference list of the Rose Report. That review had as its focus studies that provided evidence from randomised controlled trials. With these rigorous criteria it reported that:

> No statistically significant difference in effectiveness was found between synthetic phonics instruction and analytic phonics instruction and no effect of systematic phonics instruction on spelling was found. (8)

Conclusion

One must consider whether the research evidence on synthetic phonics was as strong as was suggested in the Rose Report. See chapter 14 for an evaluation of research into the issue of one best method of teaching reading, and in particular synthetic phonics. The research is more wide ranging than that cited by the Coalition Government in 2010 to justify its stance on the teaching of reading through the use of synthetic phonics, first, fast and only.

References

Buie, E. (2005) `Edict on phonics under attack,` Report of an interview with Sue Ellis *TES Scotland.* 2 September.

Education Journal (2006) `Phonics final report`. *Education Journal* Issue 94: 28.

Ellis, S. (2005) `Phonics is just the icing on the cake`. *TES Scotland.* 23 September.

House of Commons (2005) *Teaching Children to Read.* Report of the Education and Skills Select Committee. London: The Stationery Office.

Johnson, R. and Watson, J. (2005) *The effects of synthetic phonics teaching on reading and spelling attainment: a seven year longitudinal study.* On Scottish Executive website, but Insight 17 on line gives a summary.

Kelly, R. (2005) Letter to Jim Rose from The Secretary of State. 22nd June.

Marsh, J. (ed) (2005) *Popular Culture, New Media and Digital Literacy in Early Childhood.* Abingdon: RoutledgeFalmer.

Richards, C. (2006) `This could be the end of teacher autonomy`. *Education Journal.* Issue 94: 19.

Rose, J. (2005) Independent Review of the Teaching of Early Reading. Interim report online.

Rose, J. (2006) *Independent Review of the Teaching of Early Reading.* Final Report. www.standards.dfes.gov.uk/rosereview.

Torgerson, C.J., Brooks, G. and Hall, J. (2006) A Systematic *Review of the Research Literature on the use of Phonics in the Teaching of Reading and Spelling.* Research report RR711 DfES online www.dfes.gov.uk/research.

Chapter 14

Is There One Best Method of Teaching Reading: what is the research evidence?

This chapter is a revised version of an article in the *Education Journal* Issue 156, 2013: 14-16. A brief note has been added following the publication of an IMPACT pamphlet in January 2014, based on an article in the *Education Journal* Issue 188: 12-13.

Background

As early as 2005, during the last Labour Government, claims were being made for the importance of synthetic phonics as an important element in the teaching of reading. This featured in evidence to the Education and Skills Select Committee (2005) and in 2006 in the subsequently commissioned Rose Report (see previous chapter for a critique of that report).

It is important to distinguish the following:

whether there is evidence for one best method of teaching reading for all children;

whether systematic teaching of phonics should form all or at least part of children's early instruction;

whether this should be synthetic phonics rather than analytic phonics.

The coalition government in England, and Ofsted, have since 2010 stressed that the method of teaching reading should be phonics, and synthetic phonics, rather than analytic phonics, claiming this is backed by research evidence.

Definitions of phonics

Phonics instruction: Literacy teaching approaches which focus on the relationship between letters and sounds.

Systematic phonics: Teaching of letter-sound relationships in an explicit, organised and sequential fashion as opposed to incidentally or on a `when-needed` basis.

Synthetic phonics: The defining characteristics of synthetic phonics for reading are sounding-out and blending.

Analytic phonics: The defining characteristics of analytic phonics are avoiding sounding-out, and inferring sound-symbol relationships from sets of words.

(From Torgerson *et al* 2006: 8)

The evidence for one best method of teaching reading for all children will be considered, with quotations from a range of researchers, followed by an analysis of the evidence cited by the government, claimed to support synthetic phonics as the method to be used in all schools and emphasised in all courses training teachers. Finally research evidence not cited by the government will be introduced where the claims for synthetic phonics have been disputed.

Is there one best method?

As early as 1967 as shown by Jeanne Chall in *Learning to Read: the great debate,* there was extensive research and a longstanding debate about whether there was one best method of teaching reading and the controversies surrounding this. In 1972 Vera Southgate in *Beginning Reading,* commented, `I think it is highly unlikely that one method or scheme will ever prove equally effective for all pupils, being taught by all teachers, in all situations .(28) In the Bullock Report (*A Language for Life,* DES, 1975) it is stated that:

> There is no one method, medium, approach, device, or philosophy that holds the key to the process of learning to read. Too much attention has been given to polarised opinions about approaches to the teaching of reading. (521)

The report from the House of Commons Select Committee (2005) referred to above states that it is 'unlikely that any one method or set of changes would lead to a complete elimination of underachievement of reading'. (3)

More recently, in July 2011 a House of Commons All Party Parliamentary Group for Education published its Report of the Inquiry into Overcoming the Barriers to Literacy, stating that:

> Respondents were clear that there is no one panacea which guarantees all children will become readers... There are different ways to learn and different learning preferences, this is why a focus on only synthetic phonics is not appropriate. (www.educationengland.org.uk: 14).

Marilyn Adams (1990) in *Beginning to Read: thinking and learning about print,* emphasises that:

> the degree to which children internalize and use their phonic instruction depends on the degree to which they have found it useful for recognizing the words in their earliest texts...immersion – right from the start – in meaningful connected text is of vital importance. (10)

What of the research evidence on synthetic phonics?

Following the government's announcement in 2010, many experts wrote to DfE stating their concern about the insistence that in all schools in England the initial approach to teaching reading should be synthetic phonics only, also about the proposed phonics check for six-year-olds. *The Importance of Phonics: Securing Confident Reading* (www.education.gov.uk) cites researches such as several of those noted below claimed to prove the superiority of synthetic phonics as the only method for teaching reading. However, none of the researches cited below provide convincing evidence for synthetic phonics as the only approach in the early stages of learning to read.

In the previous chapter in which I critiqued the Rose Report (2006) I noted that no reference was made there to the comprehensive research by Torgerson *et al* (2006) where it is claimed that there is evidence that systematic teaching of phonics benefits children's reading accuracy, it should be part of every literacy teacher's repertoire, in a judicious balance with other elements. They also state that there is currently no strong randomised control trial evidence that any one form of systematic phonics is more effective than any other and that:

> No statistically significant difference in effectiveness was found between synthetic phonics instruction and analytic phonics instruction. (8)

In that chapter I analysed the evidence cited in the Rose Report from the Clackmannanshire study which had methodological failings, and where there was little long term gain in reading comprehension. This research and another from a Scottish local authority, West Dunbartonshire, are the researches frequently cited by the government in support of its current emphasis on synthetic phonics first, fast and only in the initial stages. However, they do not mention that in both these authorities this was part of a major intervention study with additional resources and a staff development programme (see Ellis, 2007). Sue Ellis in her article 'Policy and research: lessons from the Clackmannanshire synthetic phonics initiative', states that:

> any study driven mainly by one paradigm can only offer limited insights and that other Scottish local authorities deliberately created multi-paradigm projects in response to the national early intervention initiatives.

She also refers to the West Dunbartonshire research, claiming it as, 'possibly the most successful intervention, and based on a 'literacy for all' agenda' (294). In the final report of that research MacKay in 2007 provides an overview of the entire 10-year study. He cites the following as crucial to the success of the project:

phonological awareness and the alphabet; a strong and structured phonics emphasis; extra classroom help in the early years; raising teacher awareness; and home support for encouraging literacy through focused assessment; increased time spent on key aspects of reading; identification and support for children who are failing, and close monitoring of progress.

The project needed to be long term, have substantial funding and high levels of training of staff.

The coalition government in England cites this study as evidence for synthetic phonics, but omits to mention the above crucial elements of that research, and omits to note this final sentence in the paragraph they cite, as to whether synthetic phonics:

> has not yet been sufficiently systematically compared with better analytic phonics teaching using a faster pace and more motivating approaches. (46)

In a comprehensive research on real books versus reading schemes, Solity and Vousden (2009) analysed the structure of adult literature, children`s real books, and reading schemes, and examined the demands they make on children`s sight vocabulary and phonic skills. While they claim that learning phonic skills greatly reduces what children have to memorise, a combination of this and learning the 100 commonest sight words, and studying in the context of real books makes for `optimal instruction`. Note that these authors used the McNally and Murray 100 commonest word list from 1960s in their analysis. They still found it valuable in 2009. The authors claim that:

> the debate may be resolved by teaching an optimal level of core phonological, phonic, and sight vocabulary skills, rigorously and systematically in conjunction with the use of real books. (503)

See chapter 9 in Section II, based on a recent article, on the use of high frequency words in helping children who are learning to read. I also used the McNally and Murray 100 key words.

In 2007, Wyse and Styles in an article entitled, `Synthetic phonics and the teaching of reading: the debate surrounding England`s Rose Report`, review the international research into the teaching of early reading and claim that the Rose Report`s main recommendation on synthetic phonics contradicts the powerful body of evidence accumulated over the last 30 years`. (35)

> The conclusion of the Rose Report, that teachers and trainee teachers should be required to teach reading through synthetic phonics `first and fast` is, in our view, wrong. (41)

A further article in which the government`s view is challenged is that by Wyse and Goswami (2008). They claim that the government`s review provided no reliable empirical evidence that synthetic phonics offers the vast majority of beginners the best route to becoming skilled readers.... `There is also evidence that contextualised systematic phonics instruction is effective`. (691)

In 2012, David Reedy having explored the evidence for the quotations from Nick Gibb, Schools Minister since 2010, challenges his claims, citing contradictory evidence from Ofsted.

Footnote

IMPACT pamphlet Number 20 by Andrew Davis, `To read or not to read: decoding synthetic phonics`, was launched at a symposium in The Institute of Education in London on 29 January 2014. The pamphlet was an extended version of an article in the *Journal of Philosophy of Education* in 2012, with the title, `A monstrous regimen of synthetic phonics: fantasies of research based teaching `methods` versus real teaching`. Thus it was not surprising that before the launch of the pamphlet it had provoked controversy with several radio interviews where Davis faced up to criticism from the advocates of synthetic phonics, and with eye catching headlines in some papers.

There is not space here to give more than a flavour of the pamphlet: indeed many of the points Davis makes have been made by others. For a report on the symposium see my article in *Education Journal,* Issue 188: 13-14. Davis argues his points powerfully, and has caught the attention of the media in a way others had failed to do. He insists that there is no justification for the universal imposition of any one teaching method, and of synthetic phonics in particular. He insists that he is not opposed to phonics as such and that teachers should ensure that children learn the conventional letter sounds correspondence and that as appropriate they use such knowledge in early reading. However, he argues as have many others, that it should be suitably embedded in the context of reading for meaning` (6), and on page 7 goes on to state that if we sought to favour phonics at all we should support analytic phonics.

Davis claims that a well-established and apparently well-regarded reading programme THRASS, was deemed by DfE to be `unworthy of matched funding because it included some elements of `analytic phonics – meaning in this context at least that pupils were encouraged at times to look at whole words and how they were spelled`. (11) He expresses particular concern about the effect of this policy and the phonics check required of all 5 and 6-year-old children in England on children who can already read, referring to it as `an abuse`. He also deplores the restriction in the type of reading material by which children may now be taught in the early stages.

He argues (on page 14) that synthetic phonics, with its accompanying phonics check, at least in its pure form, fails to take account of the true character of reading and of the gulf between reading and decoding. Like others, he claims that there will inevitably be some teaching to the test with its high stakes. According to Davis, blending individual letters does not immediately result in words as such; in English for some words the reader must know the context to be able to pronounce the words. One example he cites is: `I want to tear a book. She shed a tear`. The word reading is in fact pronounced differently depending on the context and whether it refers to literacy, or a city! In 1988, I deliberately chose the title, *Reading Revisited* for my address to make this point when awarded my Fellowship by the Scottish Council for Research in Education, where the meaning was then clarified by the subtitle, `21 years of reading research`!

Davis` pamphlet was endorsed by Professor Sir Tim Brighouse, who was also a member of the panel at the launch. He endorsed it on the back cover:

> Here is a book which every primary school should have for its teachers… and if they take its lessons to heart, they will have the moral courage and the knowledge to back their own professional judgement and do what they think is right – which will not be to do as the government suggests.

At the symposium, Professor Brighouse, in his final comments widened the discussion beyond the pamphlet, to deplore the fact that in England now not only can the Secretary of State for Education tell teachers what to teach but how to teach. He worried should a medical consultant be expected to adopt a similar stance!

Conclusion

The researchers cited in this chapter support the belief that:

There is benefit from the inclusion of phonics within the early instruction in learning to read in English, within a broad programme.

There is not evidence to support phonics in isolation as the one best method.

There is not evidence for synthetic phonics as the required approach rather than analytic phonics.

In the following chapters I consider the phonics check administered to all Year One children in England for the first time in June 2012; the interim report from the National Foundation for Educational Research commissioned by DfE, unresolved issues on the validity and value of the phonics check after the second year of its administration in 2013. In addition I comment on the changes in administration of the check being introduced in 2014.

References

Adams, M. J. (1990) *Beginning to Read: thinking and learning about print.* Cambridge, Mass: MIT.

Chall, J. (1967) *Learning to Read: the great debate.* New York: McGraw-Hill.

Davis, A. (2014) `To read or not to read: decoding synthetic phonics`, *IMPACT* No.20. www.philosophy-of-education.org. Wiley.

DES (1975) *A Language for Life* (The Bullock Report). London: HMSO.

DfE (2010) *The Importance of Phonics: securing confident reading.* Online at www.education.gov.uk.

Ellis, S. (2007) `Policy and research: lessons from the Clackmannanshire synthetic phonics initiative`. *Journal of Early Childhood Literacy.* Vol 7(3): 281-297.

House of Commons (2005) *Teaching Children to Read. Report of the Education and Skills Select Committee.* London: The Stationery Office.

House of Commons (1911) *Report of the Inquiry into Overcoming the Barriers to Literacy.* London: The Stationery Office.

MacKay, T. (2007) *Achieving the Vision. The final report of the West Dunbartonshire Literacy Initiative.* (Education.centralregistry@west-dunbarton.gov.uk).

Reedy, D. (2012) `Misconceptions about teaching reading: is it only about phonics?` *Education Review.* NUT(EPC) vol. 24 (2).

Rose, J. (2006) *Independent Review of the Teaching of Early Reading.* Final Report. www.standards.dfes.gov.uk/rosereview.

Solity, J. and Vousden, J. (2009) `Real books vs reading schemes: a new perspective from instructional psychology`. *Educational Psychology.* Vol 29 (4): 469-511.

Southgate, V. (1972) *Beginning Reading.* London: University of London Press.

Torgerson, C. J., Brooks, G. and Hall, J. (2006) *A Systematic Review of the Research Literature on the use of Phonics in the Teaching of Reading and Spelling.* Research report RR711 DfES online www.dfes.gov.uk/research.

Wyse, D. and Goswami, U. (2008) `Synthetic phonics and the teaching of reading`. *British Educational Research Journal.* Vol 34 (6): 691-710.

Wyse, D. and Styles M (2007) `Synthetic phonics and the teaching of reading: the debate surrounding England`s Rose report`. *Literacy.* Vol. 41: 35-42.

NB. See also, *Whose Knowledge Counts in Government Literacy Policies? Why expertise matters,* K. S. Goodman, R. C. Calfee and Y. M. Goodman (eds), 2014. This new publication widens the discussion to include other countries including USA, Germany and France (discussed in chapter 18).

Chapter 15

The Phonics Check for all Year One Children in England:its background, results from 2012 and possible effects

This chapter is based on an article published in the *Education Journal* Issue 160, 2013: 6-8.

Background

Over the years claims have been made for one best method of teaching reading, not necessarily the same method. These claims were analysed in the previous chapter. In England the coalition government has claimed that the one best method of teaching reading is by synthetic phonics, first, fast and only, with implications for schools, the curriculum and for the training of teachers. Synthetic phonics has as its focus the relationship between letters and sounds and differs from analytic phonics in that these features are taught in isolation rather than inferring sound-symbol relationships from sets of words. In June 2012 a phonics check of 40 words (20 pseudo words and 20 real words) was administered to all Year 1 children in state schools in England for the first time. In June 2013 a similar test was administered to all Year 1 children, and to those who had failed to achieve the pass mark of 32 out of 40 the previous year. The results for both years are available and depending on which paper you read the results show either that currently two thirds of six-year-olds passed the tests this year, or that `one in three six-year-olds in England struggle with reading` (*The Guardian,* 3.10.13).

In the 2010 White Paper *The Importance of Teaching* the DfE signalled its intent to introduce a Phonics Screening Check at the end of Year 1 (to five and six-year-old pupils) in all primary schools in England - designed to be a light touch, summative assessment, including 40 words (20 real and 20 pseudo), to be read one-to-one with a teacher. The claim was that this would `identify pupils with below expected progress in phonic decoding`. Such pupils were to receive intervention, and retake the test the following year. A pilot study across 300 schools was commissioned in 2011 (*Process Evaluation of the Year 1 Phonics Screening Pilot*, 2012, www.shu.ac.uk/ceir), to help plan the administration of the check, not to decide whether it would be implemented.

Note the difference between systematic teaching of phonics and the use of either synthetic or analytic phonics teaching. The government documents emphasise synthetic phonics as the method to be used.

Initial concerns

Following the government's announcement in 2010, many experts wrote to DfE stating their concern about the insistence that in all schools the initial approach to teaching reading should be synthetic phonics only, and about the proposed phonics check. Following the first nationwide administration of the Check in June 2012, with a pass set at 32 out of 40, claimed to be the age appropriate level, further concerns were expressed at many aspects:

- the pass/fail decision resulting in many children aged between five and six years of age and their parents being told they have failed;
- the inclusion of 20 pseudo words in the test;
- the demand that the children who 'failed' retake the test the following year;
- the match-funding for schools to purchase commercial phonics materials and training courses for teachers on synthetic phonics (from a recommended list) with a monitoring of this by DfE;
- the lack of any diagnostic aspects or suggestion that other methods may be appropriate for some children who have failed;
- possible effects on some successful readers who may yet have failed this test.

According to a DfE press release, by January 2012 thousands of schools had already spent 'more than £7.7 million on new phonics products and training from a 'phonics catalogue of approved products and services'. Furthermore schools could claim up to £3000 to buy such products and training until March 2013. Nick Gibb, the schools minister, invited schools to purchase such materials, 'to improve the way they teach systematic synthetic phonics - the tried and tested method of improving the reading of our children, especially the weakest'. He reprimanded local authorities where the uptake had been low, in spite of the fact that some schools might well have had adequate supplies of materials. The match-funding was extended to October 2013.

The results of the first phonics check

The Statistical First Release of the results of the phonics screening test was published in September 2012.What was claimed as the 'expected standard of phonic decoding', namely 32 out of 40, was met by only 58% of pupils (62% of girls and 54% of boys). One must question the authority for this decision.

In the report there is a breakdown for different groups of children, showing wide variation in the pass rate:

- 62% of girls scored 32 or more but only 54% of boys;
- only 44% of those on free meals met this 'required standard';
- a comparison by date of birth reveals striking differences between the oldest and youngest children. The pass rate for the oldest boys was 65% and for the youngest (still only five years of age) was 44%; for girls the two figures were 72% and 51%;
- An even more striking finding is that, 'Travellers of Irish Heritage and those of a Gypsy/Roma background were the groups with the lowest percentages achieving the required standard in phonics, 16 and 17 per cent respectively.

Furthermore, the teachers were informed in advance that 32 out of 40 was the pass mark, pass or fail being the only recorded information. A breakdown by percentages scoring each mark reveals that while only 2% of pupils gained a mark of 31, 7% were awarded 32. This pattern is unlikely to be explained by the structure of the test; it must have been tempting to give one more mark when that meant a pass! Not only were the parents of those who `failed` informed, but the children were required to retake this test in 2013, having had further synthetic phonics instruction, with the schools `encouraged` to purchase commercial programmes. One must question whether this is the appropriate action on the basis of these results.

Having seen the actual test I became even more disturbed. The first twelve words were all pseudo words, starting with pib, vus, yop, elt, desh. What message does this give to children about reading? There is evidence from the online surveys by UKLA and the teachers` unions that some of those confused by the pseudo words were children who were already reading.

Why spend money on developing such a pass/fail test, and why test all year 1 children (about 600,000) rather than extend the use of diagnostic tests such as Reading Recovery, providing as it does diagnostic information and proven intervention strategies with long term effects?

Effects on schools, the curriculum and teacher training

On schools: UKLA and teachers` unions (ATL/NAHT/NUT) investigated the views of teachers` on the phonics check. Nine in ten Year 1 teachers said the phonics checks did not tell them anything new about the reading ability of their pupils; 86% said they should not continue, even many who had been open-minded before administering it. Nine in ten had practised reading made-up (pseudo) words and many felt under pressure to teach synthetic phonics immediately prior to the test. Good readers who had not met the criterion might have their reading materials limited on the basis of DfE recommendations and were required to re-sit the check.

Furthermore why offer £10 million for a literacy catch up programme for disadvantaged pupils who are behind in reading and writing, but only at the end of their primary school, while offering only match-funding for more commercial synthetic phonics materials and courses for children designated failures by the phonics check? It is conceivable that a different approach might be appropriate for at least some of these children, while some of the younger children who failed might have matured sufficiently to pass the test a year from now without the use of further phonics materials.

It should be noted that while the results for individual schools were not made widely available they are online for Ofsted to consult. What is disturbing is not that fact so much as the detailed analysis for individual schools with percentages compared with national figures, often based on very small numbers. For example in one school where there were only 12 children within one category and only 2 reached the required/expected standard there is a column listing that as 17% compared to the national percentage of 50%.

On the curriculum: A National Curriculum Review has been undertaken and when the draft English Key Stage 1 and 2 recommendations (for the primary schools) were published, The United Kingdom Literacy Association responded with positive comments on some recommendations, but expressed concern at a number of aspects:

- the focus on phonics, not just as one of a range of strategies;
- the recommendation that the early reading will be from `phonetically plausible texts`;
- the effects on fluent readers;
- lack of reference to home literacy practices;
- lack of reference to critical literacy or technologies.

To quote: `the soul has been taken out of the subject`.

On training: The dictates from DfE are not only having a major impact on practice in schools, removing the freedom of practitioners to adopt the approaches they think appropriate for their individual children. The recommendations by Ofsted (the inspection body in England) lay emphasis on the importance of checking that these edicts are followed in all schools, and in training institutions. HMCI Sir Michael Wilshaw, stated that

> Ofsted will sharpen its focus on phonics in routine inspections of all initial teacher education provision – primary, secondary and Further

Education. Ofsted will also start a series of unannounced inspections solely on the training of phonics teaching in providers of primary initial teacher education.` (*Education*, online No 461 16 March 2012)

DfE has commissioned the National Foundation for Educational Research to undertake an evaluation to assess whether the screening check is meeting the objectives set out by the Government. The research is funded from 2012-15. In chapter 16 the findings of the first interim report are considered.

A final note: The report of EU High Level Group of Experts on Literacy, (ec.europe.eu/education/literacy/resources/final-report), published that same year, in September 2012, carries a very different message:

Its recommendations for the primary school years include:

establish specialist reading teachers and higher qualifications for all primary teachers;

ensure that all newly qualified teachers obtain a master`s degree, with competences in, for example critical evaluation of literacy research and new instructional methods,

tailor instruction to student language diversity and engaging parents in their children`s reading and writing work at school. (91)

Chapter 16

Research Evidence on the First Phonics Check for all Year One Children in England

This chapter is based on an article in the *Education Journal*. Issue 168, 2013: 12-14.

Background

In June 2012, for the first time, a phonics screening check was administered to all Year 1 children in England. Commencing 17 June 2013 a further cohort of Year 1 children were required to sit a similar test; those children who failed to reach the required level in 2012 (32 out of 40 words correct) were also required to sit the check again. See chapter 14 for a review of the evidence claimed by the coalition government in England for synthetic phonics and chapter 15 for the results of the first administration of the Phonics Check.

The DfE commissioned the National Foundation for Educational Research (NFER) to undertake research over the period 2012-2015 to consider the impact of the check on the teaching of phonics in primary schools, on the wider literacy curriculum and on the standard of reading. The first research report was published by DfE in May 2013, *Evaluation of the Phonics Screening Check: first interim report* (M. Walker, S. Bartlett, H. Betts, M. Sainsbury and P. Mehta). Clearly by this stage only some aspects of the remit could be considered. In this chapter I will outline the findings so far and refer briefly to a research undertaken by Maggie Snowling and her colleagues, reported in the media, in press in the *Journal of Research in Reading* in 2014. I will also identify issues not considered in the available research.

The National Foundation for Educational Research interim report

Background

The interim report provides an overview of participating schools' phonics teaching practices and the emerging impact of the check. The evidence is based on case study interviews in 14 primary schools in June and July 2012, baseline surveys of 844 literacy coordinators and 940 Year 1 teachers in schools. The ways that teachers were prepared to administer the check and their confidence in administering it, the appropriateness of the check for specific groups of pupils, and ways in which the mandatory check influenced the teaching of phonics in the schools are discussed in the report.

The Executive Summary

1. Most teachers prepared themselves for the administration of the check, and many watched the online video on scoring. About half the teachers also attended external training specifically on the check.

2. The median additional financial cost incurred by schools in supporting the introduction and administration of the check is stated in the summary as £400, but with wide variation, reported later in the report as varying from zero to £5000. I suspect this is misleading, lacking details as to what individual respondents included or excluded in this figure, for example teacher time, supply cover etc. Furthermore, it does not appear to include purchase of commercial materials and training courses bought as a consequence of the implementation of the check. Any estimate of the cost effectiveness of the check must include the cost of designing this new check, of the pilot study, printing and distributing the check to all schools, the collation of the results, and the match-funding. Some idea of this may be seen in chapter 18, based on enquiries made by this author under the Freedom of Information Act.

3. The median additional time reported in supporting the introduction and administration of the check was 6 hours (with a range from zero to 40 hours

and over ten hours of senior leader time). Here also one must wonder if these questions were differently interpreted by respondents.

4. Some benefits are acknowledged, `including confirming the results of other assessments and placing an emphasis on phonics teaching`.

5. Year 1 teachers had mixed views on the standard of the check with slightly more suggesting it was too difficult.

6. Issues are raised about the suitability of the check for certain groups of pupils. This included not only pupils with special educational needs but also high ability pupils and those with English as an additional language.

7. Information on communication with parents was collected very shortly after the administration of the check, thus in most cases the respondents were only reporting how they intended to communicate the results to parents/carers rather than what they had actually done.

8. A third of the schools reported making changes to phonics teaching in anticipation of the check, increasing assessment, increasing time and starting to use phonics programmes more systematically. It had also stimulated discussion between Year 1 and Year 2 teachers.

9. Views on the value of the check seemed contradictory depending on the way questions were framed, since one of the key messages to emerge was that:

> Many schools appear to believe that a phonics approach to teaching reading should be used alongside other methods.

> However, it is less certain that this is an endorsement of the recommended approach of systematic synthetic phonics taught first and fast.

> While nine out of ten literacy coordinators agree, at least to some extent that systematic teaching of phonics has value in the primary

classroom ..., a similar proportion feel that a variety of different methods should be used to teach children to decode words. (8)

It is open to debate why the staff interviewed have not fully endorsed the government's approach, whether from confusion or from conviction! (See also pages 19-20 and 23 in the report). It is commented that a third of survey respondents felt in some way that phonics has too high a priority in current education policy.

10. When questions were asked specifically about the check, rather than the value of phonics in the teaching of reading, attitudes were more varied. Many were negative, and a few positive, while others regarded it as 'broadly acceptable but unnecessary'. The researchers query whether respondents may not have been fully aware of the rationale behind the introduction of the check. This does not appear to be explored further in this report

Phonics teaching practices

This section explores current practices and changes made because of the phonics check. Most Year 1 and Year 2 teachers reported that phonics teaching took place daily and on average two hours per week. All case study schools also indicated a strong school focus on phonics, with daily phonics sessions for children from Foundation Stage through to at least Year 2 by most. The indication was that around 90 per cent of schools taught in discrete phonics sessions in Reception, Years 1 and 2, while for some it was integrated in other work. Letters and Sounds and Jolly Phonics are the most frequently mentioned core programmes. Almost half the respondents referred to their school being involved in externally provided training specifically focused on the teaching of phonics. Some schools had sent teaching assistants on such training as well as class teachers. This was often supplied by local authorities with some training supplied by commercial training providers, the most frequently mentioned being Read, Write Inc. (See chapter 18 for nation-wide information on this aspect).

Given the level of training, external and in-house it is not surprising that most respondents thought their teachers were well prepared.

Results

The results in the schools where the Year 1 teachers completed the survey were comparable to the national average (61 per cent pass, 58 per cent nationally). Few pupils were `disapplied` (usually at most one pupil), meaning they did not sit the check. In a few cases the testing was stopped when a child was beginning to struggle or becoming distressed.

Conclusions in the report

When asked directly, only two case-study schools said they could see some benefit to the check. The teachers had mixed views on the level of difficulty of the check and most teachers felt the check was not suitable for children with speech, language or communication needs and children with other learning difficulties. Reference was made by some to problems with pseudo words which distracted some of these children. In some cases the children struggled to communicate their answers clearly. The views were more mixed with regard to the appropriateness of the check for children with EAL. Here also problems with pseudo words are mentioned.

The survey found Year 1 teachers held mixed views concerning the suitability of the check for independent and fluent readers (40% regarded it as unsuitable and 22% very unsuitable). In only seven of fourteen case study schools had the parents/carers been notified in advance of the administration of the check. Further information will be required as to exactly in what form and in how much detail parents/carers have now been informed of the results, as not all schools would yet have provided this information by the time of this survey. Many suggested this information would form part of end of year written reports. Some teachers expressed concern at branding some children as failures; others had concerns about what to communicate as well as how.

Many interviewees reported no substantial changes to teaching but those who did mention changes indicated:

- A greater focus on pseudo words;
- more phonetic spelling tests rather than high frequency words;

- parental workshops on phonics;
- revision sessions in preparation for the check;
- an increase in the number of phonics sessions.

Key messages from the report

Among the key messages at the end of the report are the following:

- Many schools appear to believe that a phonics approach to teaching reading should be used alongside other methods.
- Most teachers are positive about the importance of phonics teaching.

It is less certain that this is an endorsement of the recommended approach of systematic synthetic phonics taught first and fast. While the researchers raise the possibility that there is widespread misunderstanding of the term, this is only one possible explanation.

Further comments

There seems to have been no discussion with the teachers of analytic versus the recommended synthetic phonics. There is surprisingly little reference to the age of the children, though some respondents did mention the younger children still only five years of age. Also surprisingly little reference is made to the inclusion of pseudo words in the check. It is to be hoped that issues such as these will be explored further in subsequent reports.

However, most teachers interviewed as part of the case-study visits to schools reported that, *the check would have minimal, if any, impact on the standard of reading and writing in their school in the future*. (7) Italics not in original.

Further research evidence: Phonics test `accurate but unnecessary` (BBC News 5.6.13 online)

A research directed by Maggie Snowling of Oxford University criticises the phonics check on the basis that it has no prescribed course of action. The researchers measured pupils` scores in the phonics check against regular phonics checks and other standardised reading and spelling tests. They conclude that while the government test was accurate in identifying children who were struggling, it offered no information that teacher assessment did not already provide. They claim that the check tended to over-estimate the number of at-risk readers. I had the opportunity to study the unpublished report of this research. This will appear in the *Journal of Research in Reading* in 2014.: `The phonics check: is it valid, sensitive and necessary`, (F.J. Duff, S.E. Mengoni, A.M. Bailey, and M.J. Snowling). It should be noted that Maggie Snowling and Alison Bailey were among the five experts involved in the independent review of the assessment framework, (see chapter 18).

Unresolved issues

These two researches raise issues about the costs and benefits of a one off test versus further training for teachers to monitor children`s progress. There may be a faulty logic in a one-off pass/fail test:

- where the child reaches or fails to reach an arbitrary prescribed standard;
- is vastly expensive to develop and administer;
- may over-estimate those at- risk;
- is not diagnostic and where there is no specific funding linked to the needs of individual children, other than commercial synthetic phonics programmes that follows the identification of children who are struggling.

The children`s voices

Lacking so far is any assessment of the effects of these developments on young children`s experiences of and attitudes towards literacy. How will this greater emphasis on phonics in the early stages, the isolated nature of much of their tuition in phonics, the new emphasis on pseudo words and the phonics check itself influence their understanding of the nature of literacy and attitude to reading? We need to interview the children and gain insight into their views, including those who passed the check, any who could read but failed the check and those who were required to re-sit the following year.

Finally, what messages are we giving parents on how to help their young children to become literate and to value the written word?

Chapter 17

Unresolved Issues on the Value and Validity of the Phonics Check: three years on

This chapter is based on an article in the *Education Journal*. Issue 177, 2013: 13-15. Information has been added on changes in the phonics check in 2014, from the guidance notes for administration of the check in 2014, published in February 2014, see www.education.gov.uk/ks1.

Background

In the 2010 White Paper *The Importance of Teaching*, the DfE signalled its intent to introduce a Phonics Screening Check at the end of Year 1 (to five and six- year-old pupils) in all primary schools in England - designed to be a light touch, summative assessment, including 40 words (20 real and 20 pseudo), to be read one-to-one with a teacher. The claim was that this would `identify pupils with below expected progress in phonic decoding`. Such pupils were to receive intervention, and retake the test the following year. Synthetic phonics, the approach required by the government, has as its focus the relationship between letters and sounds and differs from analytic phonics in that these features are taught in isolation rather than inferring sound-symbol relationships from sets of words. Many experts expressed concern about the proposed phonics check, as shown in chapters 14 and 15.

In the previous three chapters I considered; the lack of research evidence for the claim that synthetic phonics is the one best method of teaching reading (chapter 14); the results of the first check administered in June 2012 (chapter 15) and the interim results of the NFER research commissioned by DfE (chapter 16). The results of the second administration of the check in June 2013 will here be compared with those from 2012. Many issues still remain unresolved concerning the check, its format, the scoring and its implications for practice. It will be interesting to discover which if any of these have been addressed in 2014.

In June 2012 the phonics check was administered to all Year 1 children in state funded schools in England for the first time. In June 2013 a similar test was administered to all Year 1 children and to those in Year 2 who had failed to achieve the pass mark of 32 out of 40 the previous year or to whom it had not been administered.

A few changes have been made for 2014 according to the Administrators' Guide for 2014, including a decision not to reveal the threshold mark in advance as in the previous two years. However, this will be published online on 30 June, a few days after the testing is completed. Schools will need to know it to enable them to decide whether a child has passed or failed and to complete their returns, as pass/fail is still the reported information. No explanation has so far been given for this decision. It does deal with concerns about the peak in percentages of children achieving 32, the threshold mark, in the two previous years. However, it will be interesting to see how the threshold mark is determined, and how 2014 percentages of children achieving the threshold can legitimately be compared with the previous two years.

Among the changes listed for 2014 is the inclusion of 'maintained nursery schools with registered children who will reach the age of six before the end of the school year'. It is also noted that 'children who were not assessed at all at the end of Year 1, as well as those who did not meet the standard at the end of Year 1, are now included in the phonics screening check retakes policy'. For a light touch assessment the security recommended to the schools is astonishingly rigorous as schools are advised to 'Conduct regular checks of the materials to ensure they have not been tampered with'! It is not clear whether in 2014 the check will still begin with twelve pseudo words, as all that is stated is that there will be four words per page, and that real and pseudo words will not be on the same page. See *Check Administrators' Guide* on www.education.gov.uk/ks1.

Concerns about the phonics check

Following the first nationwide administration of the Check in June 2012, concerns were expressed that:

- The pass/fail decision resulted in many children aged between five and six years of age and their parents being told they had failed;
- the inclusion of 20 pseudo words in the test;
- the structure of the test, with the first twelve words all pseudo words;
- coloured illustrations, referred to as `types of imaginary creatures`, to distinguish the pseudo words;
- the lack of any diagnostic aspects;
- the fact that the pass mark was known in advance by teachers;
- the demand that the children who `failed` retake the test the following year;
- the effect on some successful readers who may yet have failed this test.

Match-funding for schools had been available from September 2011 until October 2013 to purchase commercial phonics materials and training courses for teachers on synthetic phonics (from a limited recommended list). The costs of this aspect will be discussed in chapter 18.

A comparison of the results of the phonics checks in 2012 and 2013

Results for 2012

The Statistical First Release of the results of the phonics screening test was published in September 2012. What was claimed as the `expected standard of phonic decoding`, namely 32 out of 40, was met by only 58% of pupils. However, there was wide variation in the percentages passing within different groups of children (62% of girls scored 32 or more but only 54% of boys) and only 44% of those on free meals met this `required standard`. Although there was a year's difference between the youngest and oldest children tested, information on this was not available from published tables. I requested this information and, as I anticipated, found there was a wide discrepancy, with the pass rate for the oldest boys 65% and for the youngest (still only five years of age) 44%; for girls the two figures were 72% and 51%.

An even more disturbing feature was that a breakdown by percentages scoring each mark revealed, that while only 2% of pupils gained a mark of 31, 7% were awarded 32, a pattern unlikely to be explained by the structure of the test. In chapter 15, and in my article, I drew attention to this anomaly, commenting that this pass mark was known in advance to the teachers, that the structure of the actual test could not have explained this distribution, and that it must have been tempting to give 32 rather than 31 when this made the difference between a pass and a fail. In view of the change for 2014, when the threshold mark will not be known in advance, it will be interesting to learn how any changes in percentages of children achieving the threshold mark are interpreted.

Schools were required to inform parents of the results, that is whether their children passed or failed. Those who `failed` were required to retake a similar test in 2013, presumably after further synthetic phonics instruction over the ensuing year, with the schools `encouraged` to purchase more commercial programmes. It is also likely that these children will have practised similar tests, including pseudo words.

Results of phonics check for 2013

The test for 2013 was similar to the previous year, again with the first twelve words pseudo words (with coloured illustrations). The pass mark again was 32 out of 40 and again the teachers were informed in advance that 32 is the pass mark. To quote:

> This mark was communicated to schools in advance of the screening check being administered so that schools could immediately put in place extra support for pupils who had not met the required standard.

The results for 2013 are to be found at: www.gov.uk/government/statistics-key-stage-1. The pattern is similar to 2012, but with 69% meeting the expected standard, an increase of 11% since 2012; as previously girls outperformed boys. The results for Year 2 are presented nationally by pupil characteristics and include a local authority summary. By the end of Year 2 in 2013 85% of pupils (typically aged 7) met the expected standard. This includes those who passed in Year 1 in 2012, those retaking the check in 2013 and any taking the test for the first time in 2013. This is claimed to represent an increase of 27 percentage points from 58%.

In 2013 I again requested information by date of birth. The relevant figures for Year 1 children in 2013 are 75% for the oldest boys and 55% for the youngest, and 81% and 64% for the girls. Again one might question whether the younger children might by the following year have matured sufficiently to pass the test without further synthetic phonics. No reference has been made to this in DfE statements so far.

Yet again in 2013 there was a `spike` at mark 32, known in advance to be the pass mark, with one per cent of children scoring 31 and 7% scoring 32. I had drawn attention to this anomaly in the previous year`s results. The findings from the first interim report from the NFER research commissioned by DfE were analysed in chapter16; these only took account of the first year`s testing. I had initially failed to note, a significant comment by NFER based on the 2012 results in Topic Note: 2012 Phonics Screening Check: research report May 2013, (L.Townley and D. Cotts) where they are more specific in their interpretation of these results, referring to:

> a spike at the threshold of meeting the expected standard, *suggesting that pupils on the borderline may have been marked up.* [my italics].

> By removing pupils` scores around the spike and using regression techniques, it is estimated that 46% of pupils would meet the expected standard if there was not a spike at the borderline` (28). [that is instead of 58%]

Since the administration of the check was similar in 2013, with the pass mark known in advance, it seems likely that yet again the numbers of pupils passing the check have been over estimated. There may also be differences between schools, or markers, in the extent to which borderline pupils have been marked up. This makes the whole exercise even more questionable. Were the pass mark not to be divulged in advance this effect might be minimised; however, it would no longer be possible to compare results from one year to the next. In the light of comments such as this I was interested to note that the threshold mark will not in 2014 be revealed in advance.

Value and validity of the check

The NFER research interim report has already raised issues about the costs and benefits of a one off test versus teachers being well trained to monitor children's progress. There may be a faulty logic in a one-off pass/fail test, where the child reaches or fails to reach an arbitrary prescribed standard, a mark known to the teachers in advance, a test that is vastly expensive to develop and administer, which may over-estimate those at-risk, is not diagnostic and where there is no specific funding linked to identified needs of individual children that follows the identification of children who are struggling. The following are relevant:

- No clear rationale has been provided for identifying the mark of 32 as meeting the expected standard;
- no clear explanation has been given for the inclusion of pseudo words in the test;
- no analysis has been undertaken of the contribution of the pseudo words to the final scores, yet more latitude is permitted in pronunciation of pseudo words than the real words;
- the evidence of a spike in percentage of children gaining a mark of 32 rather than 31 in both years of administration of the test, a pass mark known to the teachers in advance, raises serious questions about the validity of this test;
- the implications of a large difference in pass rate between the youngest and oldest children needs to be considered;
- the needs of those who failed to reach the arbitrary pass mark on this test may not be met by a focus on synthetic phonics as the solution to their problems.

Costing the policy on synthetic phonics

It is disturbing how much money and time has been devoted to a detailed analysis of the results of this test which by most standards of test construction seems flawed, including a breakdown by types of schools and by local authorities. Furthermore detailed results for individual schools are available at RAISEonline, accessible to Ofsted as evidence for inspections, including percentages within the various categories (often based on very small numbers) then compared with national percentages.

It has yet to be established just what effect this policy is having on the literacy experiences of young children in state schools in England. We need among other things to talk with the young children themselves, those who are failing and those who were already well on the way to becoming successful readers, to examine their opinions of the experience of the check and the extent to which it is colouring their views on literacy. In chapter 18 the cost of the commercial phonics programmes and training courses schools have been encouraged to purchase with funding from DfE will be reported. The discussion there will be widened to include experiences in other countries, including US, Germany and France.

Chapter 18

Whose Knowledge Counts in Government Literacy Policies: at what cost?

The first part of this chapter is based on an article in the *Education Journal* Issue 186, 2014: 13-16. The evidence for the second apart is from *Whose Knowledge Counts in Government Literacy Policies? Why expertise matters,* K. S. Goodman, R. C. Calfee and Y. M. Goodman (eds). 2014. New York: Routledge.

Background

In the previous chapter I questioned the cost of the commercial phonics programmes and training courses for teachers that schools were encouraged to purchase, with additional funding from DfE between September 2011 and October 2013. I noted that only selected programmes and training courses were available for such funding. The information I was able to secure under the Freedom of Information Act forms the first part of this chapter. In the second part of the chapter the discussion is widened to include information from The United States, France, Germany and developing countries where similar developments involving commercial programmes have taken place. This section draws on evidence from relevant parts of *Whose Knowledge Counts in Government Literacy Policies? Why expertise matters,* K. S. Goodman, R. C. Calfee and Y. M. Goodman (eds), 2014, New York: Routledge.

Part 1 Costing the synthetic phonics policy in England

Match-funding for commercial programmes and training courses on synthetic phonics

Over the period September 2011 to October 2013 DfE made match-funding available for schools that either purchased commercial materials or training courses from 'The Importance of Phonics' catalogue. The match-funding programme was managed for the government by a group of five organisations known as Pro5; an agreed commission was included in the catalogue sale price.

1. Over that period a total of £23,593,109 match-funding was provided for schools, approximately £22 million for materials and a further £1.3 million for training courses. As the schools could only claim up to 50% of their total expenditure on the phonics materials or training from match-funding, at least a similar amount was spent by schools. Furthermore this only covers expenditure during that period, and only on the materials on the list issued by the government.

2. The claim for the commercial programmes was approximately £19 million (excluding VAT), but it was possible to obtain a breakdown by programme for only Mainstream Programmes, accounting for about £11 million of the match-funding for programmes. The other categories were Supplementary Resources (£3.5 million), Supplementary Resources Decodable Readers (£3.7 million), Phonics Catch-up Schemes (£501,000) and Phonics Catch-up Supplementary Resources (£108,000). The three programmes receiving the largest amount of the £11 million were Read Write Inc. (over £4 million), Phonics Bug (nearly £4 million) and Floppy Phonics (approx. £3 million). Four other programmes were listed as receiving the rest of the money. It was stated in the response I had from DfE that, `schools were free to choose which products and/or training to purchase from the Catalogue independently of the Government`.

3. A breakdown of those receiving the largest amounts within the training programme of approximately £1.095,733 showed that £546,614 went to Ruth Miskin Literacy Ltd, Sounds Write Ltd received £129,734 and Ann Foster Literacy £73,654. The remaining 27 providers listed received the rest of the money.

4. Over the period September 2011 to October 2013 when match-funding was available, it was claimed by 14,263 schools (233 for training only and 1697 for training and products).

Some other costs of the phonics check

I also asked further questions under the Freedom of Information Act concerning the cost of elements of the phonics check and about those involved in the development of the check. The answers to these are as follows for 2012 and 2013 taken together:

Distribution to schools including printing and collating   £458,000

Guidance products £217,000

Item level data collection £176,000

Main data collection and production of the statistical first release   £63,000

The total over the two years was noted as £914,000 plus £300,000 for the pilot survey. There would in addition be the cost of the NFER research commissioned by DfE. Not included in these figures are any of the additional costs to schools in administering the phonics check.

Who were the experts consulted?

I asked for the names of those who were responsible for devising the phonics check. I was informed that as the answer to that question was `already reasonably accessible` DfE were not required to provide it under the Freedom of Information Act. However, I was directed to: http://media.education.gov.uk/assets/files/pdf2/phonics%202011%20technical%20report.pdf.

That publication is the *Year 1 Phonics screening check Pilot 2011: Technical Report* of 131 pages. On page 11 of that it is stated that` the pilot framework was initially developed in conjunction with four leading phonics experts: Jenny Chew; Ruth Miskin; Rhona Stainthorp and Morag Stuart`.

On page 18 the following experts are listed as involved in the independent review of the assessment framework: Alison Bailey, Bryan Byrne, Rhona Johnston, Maggie Snowling and Janet Vousden. I was informed that, `The test was constructed by test development experts within STA following the pilot, including test development researchers and psychometricians, to meet the specification`.

From the detailed technical report I was not able to establish who was responsible for several of the aspects of the final check that I and others criticised. It was clear that the experts named supported the use of pseudo words. However, from this detailed report it is still not clear who decided:

- To make the first twelve words of the check all pseudo words;
- to inform the teachers in advance of the pass mark of 32 out of 40;
- to restrict the information made available (including to parents) to a pass/fail;
- for the lack of diagnostic information from the test, and
- that those who scored less than 32 retake the test the following year.

I wonder whether any of these decisions caused concern to any of the independent experts consulted for the pilot study.

I acknowledge the help I received from DfE and the detailed answers prepared for me under The Freedom of Information Act. Clearly these costs are only `the tip of the iceberg` as they do not take account of materials or training courses purchased before or after the match-funding initiative and other costs to the schools in administering the phonics check. There will also have been costs to institutions involved in training teachers, as they are required to give synthetic phonics a high profile in their training courses. Many such institutions will have purchased commercial programmes and/or employed synthetic phonics experts as trainers on their courses.

Part II A wider perspective on the commercialisation of literacy policies

The book, *Whose Knowledge Counts in Government Literacy Policies? Why expertise matters* (Goodman *et al*, 2014) is in two parts: Part I The Political Realities and Part II Aspects of Literacy: the knowledge base. Part II explores many important aspects of literacy teaching, including the curriculum, text complexity, the role of children`s literature, diversity in

174

children's literature and the roles of writing teachers. Part I is the focus here, however, as it extends the discussion beyond what is happening in England and reveals similar concerns among professionals in other countries about who determines literacy policies and at what cost. The chapters in Part I of Goodman *et al* are as follows:

Kenneth Goodman: Whose Knowledge Counts? The pedagogy of the absurd (chapter 2);

Patrick Shannon: Re-reading poverty; reorienting educational policy (chapter 3);

Jacques Fijalkow: Neoliberal and Neoconservative literacy education policies in contemporary France (chapter 4);

Henrietta Dombey: Flying blind: government policy on the teaching of reading in England and research on effective literacy education (chapter 5);

Sue Ellis: Whose knowledge counts, for whom, in what circumstances? The ethical constraints on who decides (chapter 6);

Renate Valtin: About the dubious role of phonological awareness in the discussion of literacy policies (chapter 7).

As chapters 5 and 6 refer directly to policy in England and in Scotland I will consider these first. In chapter 5, Henrietta Dombey critiques the current coalition government policy on synthetic phonics in England discussed in the previous chapters. She places this in a wider context, stressing that we are enduring a policy that is likely to be counter-productive and that:

> The challenge for the future is to change this state of affairs, by persistently calling attention to research and practice in England, and to the experiences of our colleagues elsewhere in the world. (76)

Sue Ellis, in chapter 6, while contrasting the position in England with that in Scotland, stresses that:

Literacy educators and researchers are finding themselves in an increasingly tangled political and legal landscape, where frameworks that help to locate what evidence really means in the context of complex interventions are extremely important. (90)

In chapter 4, Jacques Fijalkow points out that France has a highly centralised state system; programmes are decided in Paris and `imposed throughout the country by means of an impressive array of training and control policies` (47). He deplores the fact that those whose knowledge should count does not also count.

First, in spite of over 100 years of data collection and studies, research from the human and social sciences....... is not valued at all also, Second teachers` knowledge does not count either...... Clearly there is an irony that leaves an important question unanswered. How do people with knowledge that should count make themselves heard? (65)

In chapter 7, Renate Valtin cites similar concerns in Germany where politicians prefer the advice of those who offer simplistic solutions, ignoring the wealth of research available. On page 96, for example, she questions whether there is sufficient empirical evidence on phonological awareness for it to be regarded as the strongest predictor of learning written language in alphabetic orthographies, and on page 99, she stresses that: `The task of segmenting words into sounds or phonemes is very difficult`. She expresses concern that preschool programmes in Germany disregard linguistic and educational knowledge about emergent literacy in school. Her final comment is:

In kindergarten, time should be devoted to oral language development and to experiences with the *functions* of written language by providing a rich literacy environment. (106)

I have deliberately left until last the insights from chapter 2 by Kenneth Goodman. Although part of it concerns tracing the development of the programmes holding sway in The United States and how this power developed, there are also many important points of universal concern. He states that:

> While there are still major differences among researchers, the issues that should be the ones being debated are not the ones politicians and the press are highlighting. (23)

He refers to a small group of new neo-conservatives whose mission is to control the curriculum. The following quote seems to resonate well beyond The United States:

> Their strategy is to frame the campaign as reform of a failing educational system. They chose to attack reading methodology and write into law a simplistic phonics model as a key to making public education appear to be failing. They are responsible for the emphasis on testing, the labelling of schools, and the punishments, which are designed to lead to their privatization. (26)

Part of Goodman's chapter is devoted to the development and spread of a particular screening test DIBELS (Dynamic Indicators of Basic Early Learning Literacy Skill), a series of sub-tests each of which takes only one minute to administer. One sub-test is a test of the ability to sound out nonsense digraphs and trigraphs, the premise being that the best test of phonics is non-words where meaning doesn't get in the way of the phonics. However, Goodman claims that there is widespread agreement among reading authorities and psychometricians that DIBELS is a very bad test, yet the test is administered three times a year and those who fail are taught the skills of the test and retested. He notes a conflict of interest as the authors of that test were sitting on committees judging applications by states for funds, and making the adoption of the test a condition of approval for state funding. He discusses the effects of such tests on the curriculum and on teachers and reports a further worrying development. A similar test EGRA (early grade reading assessment) has been developed and translated into English, French, Spanish and several native languages. He claims that DIBELS showed little linguistic sophistication in its construction and that

177

EGRA (early grade reading assessment) did not go beyond that. The story becomes even more disturbing, as not only was this test used in developing countries, but, in Senegal, according to Goodman, where the home language is French for only 2% of the pupils, they were tested in French!

Final comments

As may be seen from the information cited above England is not the only country where evidence from research is being ignored, simplistic tests are driving the curriculum, available resources for schools are being spent on commercial products linked to the tests and schools are being ranked on the basis of such tests. In the words of Fijalkow:

`How do people with knowledge that should count make themselves heard?`

Section V
Interpretations of Literacies in the Twenty-first Century

A number of international reports on attainment have been published in recent years. The assessment of 10-year-olds in 35 countries for the PIRLS report discussed in Chapter 19 was undertaken in 2001 and published in 2003. The focus here is on the sampling and interpretation of the results and on claims made by politicians and the media on the basis of the results. More recently further reports have been published, including PISA, on the attainment of 15-year-olds in 2009 in 65 countries, and 2012 in 64 countries. Following this more recent report both the media and politicians have again made claims as to how the findings should be interpreted and what actions should follow, on this occasion because of a claimed fall in the standing of the United Kingdom in the international league. See the *Education Journal* Issue 184 2013 where a number of articles are devoted to an analysis of the most recent PISA report. There are lessons to be learnt from my detailed analysis of the earlier report, revealing as it does the limitations even of a carefully conducted study such as this with all the resources at its disposal. This chapter is an adapted version of an article published in the *Education Journal* in 2003 and is published here with permission from Education Publishing.

Chapter 20 is a shortened and edited version of chapter 5 in *Improving the Quality of Childhood in Europe,* 2012, vol 3, C. Clouder, B. Heys, M. Matthes and P. Sullivan (eds), based on a paper presented in Brussels in 2011. It is included here with the permission of the editors.

In chapter 21 the complexities of written language and in particular the English language are explored further. The focus in this book, and in much research, has been on learning to read in English. The discussion is widened to include other languages and orthographies.

Chapter 19

International Studies of Reading, such as PIRLS: a cautionary tale

This chapter is an edited version of an article in the *Education Journal,* Issue 75 in 2003: 25-27.

Background

PIRLS, The Progress in International Reading Literacy Study, conducted in 2001 and reported in 2003, generated headlines highlighting how well Britain was doing in that international study. One reason might be that England was ranked high among the 35 countries involved in the study, for reading for literary experience, and for acquiring and using information. Typical headlines were, 'English rank third in world reading chart' (TES), or 'English primary pupils are among the best readers in the world', and 'the most successful English-speaking country' (DfES).Yet there were startling differences between England and Scotland. In this chapter I analyse the extent to which the results were caused by the survey rather than the children surveyed.

The sample

The target population for the study was:

All students enrolled in the upper of the two adjacent grades that contain the largest proportion of 9-year-olds at the time of testing. In most countries this was Fourth Grade with an average age of 10.3 years.

In England and in Scotland these children were in their fifth year in primary school and the average ages at the time of testing were respectively 10.2 and 9.8 years. Thus most of these children would have started primary school in 1996 and have learned to read before the National Literacy Strategy commenced in England. The range of average ages in the different countries in the survey varied from about 9.7 to 11.2 (the mean age in Sweden, the highest performing country was 10.8). The tests were specifically designed for the study. In addition to the assessment of reading achievement, questionnaires were completed by the pupils, their teachers, head teachers and parents.

In most countries the sample of schools was drawn from the whole country, with approximately 150 schools in the initial sample and about 3,000 pupils. Where schools did not agree to participate, first and even second replacement schools were selected. Should the sample not meet certain criteria this is indicated in the tables and, if after first and second replacements they still did not meet the requirements, these figures are not listed in order in the tables. Very small schools and special schools were excluded, as were certain pupils within the sampled classes.

The results

The international results were published in 2003 and are available on the internet (Mullis *et al,* 2003). A separate report for England was published by the National Foundation for Educational Research which was responsible for the research conducted in England (Twist *et al*, 2003a). A summary of the latter report is also to be found in (Twist *et al*, 2003b). Media coverage was extensive, and press releases were issued by DfES. No separate report was available for Scotland, where the Scottish Executive was responsible for the research.

There was extensive coverage of the main results; therefore these will not be discussed in any detail. Attention will be on specific aspects of the sampling which may have implications for comparisons between countries and any policy decisions that might be considered as a consequence of the findings.

The basis for this chapter is the following step-by-step study of PIRLS

- Reading of the various media and press reports that were released as the results appeared;
- a detailed study of the International Report;

182

- a study of the report by NFER of the study as conducted in England;
- response to questions posed to the NFER team and to the Scottish Executive.

When studying the International Report, I took as my focus comparison of the results for England and Scotland. With some knowledge of developments in both countries before and after devolution, including the National Literacy Strategy in England, I was alert to any surprising differences between the results for these two countries. This led me to further detective work when studying the NFER report where there was more detail on the precise nature of the sampling in England; in particular I paid attention to the appendices. In some instances where I still felt the need for more information, I contacted the NFER, raising specific points. I then contacted the Scottish Executive with similar questions about the Scottish sample. I am grateful to both NFER and the Scottish Executive for their co-operation. I also refer in this chapter to the Swedish sampling patterns, as Sweden was the highest performing of all 35 countries.

An analysis of the sampling

Four aspects will be studied in detail, namely:

1) Relative participation rate of sampled schools

2) Response rate to the various questionnaires

3) Questioning of head teachers and parents with regard to reading readiness and literacy materials in the homes

4) Information on aspects of behaviour within the sampled schools.

Sampling within countries

The school participation rates before replacements were as follows:

England   57 per cent

Scotland   76 per cent

Sweden   97 per cent

In England, of the 150 schools selected, only 88 agreed to participate. It took 38 first replacement schools and for large schools a further 5 schools to achieve the final sample of 131 schools. Extremely small schools and special schools were excluded. The final sample thus met only the second category; therefore the results were included in the tables with a sign to indicate the need for replacement schools. NFER reported that after the study the SATs results for the participating schools were compared with the national results; this showed that the achieved sample was comparable to a national sample as far as achievement was concerned. I enquired of NFER what the definition of small schools was in England and was informed that schools with fewer than eight pupils in the target age group were excluded. In England about 14 per cent of pupils are in schools of fewer than 100 pupils. There were a number of exclusions from the target within school groups, including children with statements of special educational needs and those with limited facility in English, also a number of absentees.

In Scotland, in the participating sample of 118 schools there were 113 schools from the main sample, five replacement schools, and no second replacement schools. Special schools, Gaelic medium schools and very small schools (with fewer than five pupils) were excluded. These account for 3.8 per cent of the target population in Scotland.

As Sweden achieved a high participation rate from the initially sampled schools no entries for that country are asterisked in the report. Of 146 schools involved, only four were replacement schools. Thus there seems no reason to question the high standing of that country in the results.

Response to the Questionnaires

Questionnaires for students, teachers and head teachers

As was noted above questionnaires were prepared for the pupils, their class teachers and their head teachers. In most countries, including England,

Scotland and Sweden, the response rates to these questionnaires was high, over 90 per cent.

However, my interest was aroused when studying the appendix to the NFER report on England where details of the types of school are listed. In the English sample there were infant, primary, junior and middle schools as well as independent schools. It occurred to me that only the primary school heads could have responded appropriately to questions about reading readiness of the majority of children beginning primary school. Following my enquiries, I learned that only the head teachers of primary schools in England were asked these questions; this amounted to only 91 of 124 head teachers who responded to the questionnaire. In Scotland in contrast, all the schools in the study were primary schools; thus all the head teachers could appropriately have responded to these questions.

Parent questionnaires

The response rates to the parent questionnaires were as follows:
England 55 per cent (one of the lowest)

Scotland 63 per cent

Sweden 92 per cent

The response rates for some countries to the parental questionnaires were also high. However, the parental questionnaire returns for England and Scotland were low, barely acceptable to be entered in the tables. The NFER report repeatedly draws attention to this. However, this raises serious questions where evidence is based only on the parents' responses. It seems unlikely that such parents would be typical; it is more likely that they were more interested, provided more literacy related activities in the homes and had higher levels of literacy than the rest of the parents. Yet, England is singled out in the International Report for the amount of support provided by parents, and for other aspects where the information came only from the parents.

It is thus possible that the differential response rates to the questionnaire from parents in England and Scotland may provide more favourable responses concerning aspects of home support than those from other countries such as Sweden, where the coverage of parents' views and backgrounds was more representative. In view of this one must regard with some caution the finding that:

> Highest levels of engagement were reported in England and Scotland`, where more than 80 per cent of students had parents reporting often engaging in literacy related activities before their child began school (see Mullis *et al*: 96).

Attainment on entry to school

I noted earlier that major, unexpected differences between England and Scotland in some tables alerted me to seek explanations. I found there were such differences between England and other countries, including Scotland, in the reported knowledge of print on entry to primary school. While one source of this information was the parent questionnaire, another was the head teachers and their expectations of the majority of children entering their schools. Particular attention is drawn in the International Report to the high level of readiness and awareness of print of children on beginning school in England. I noted above that only a proportion of the head teachers in England were asked this question.

The difference between England and all other countries is so striking that it puzzled me, especially as it was based not only on the parents' responses but also those of the head teachers.

The heading for Table 5.4 reads: `Students in Schools Where Principals Estimate That Most Students (More than 75%) Begin School with Specific Early Literacy Skill (Mullis *et al*: 134).

The results given for England and Scotland are as follows.

:

Percentage of students attending such schools who can -	England	Scotland
recognise most letters of the alphabet	58%	2%
read some words	64%	2%
read sentences	29%	1%
write letters of the alphabet	55%	5%
write some words	44%	1%

When studying the appendix to the NFER report I noticed that the question asked in England was:

'About how many of the children in your school can do the following when they begin year 1?' (Twist *et al*: 91).

I had interpreted the findings in the International Report as referring to children beginning primary school, which is how the tables are headed. I therefore raised this with NFER and it was confirmed that the question to head teachers and parents referred to entry to Primary 1 as I had suspected, not to Reception Class. On raising the matter with colleagues in Scotland they confirmed that the question asked there was:

'About how many of the pupils in your school can do the following when they begin their first year?' This would refer to Primary 1.

Thus the questions asked in England and Scotland referred to a different class, since in Scotland children's first experience of education in a primary school is in Primary 1. Children in England enter Reception Class, prior to entering Year 1, and may well have had literacy experiences during that time.

Admittedly the children entering statutory education in most European countries are older than those in Scotland and England. However, attention had already been drawn to that point in the report. Thus it seems wrong to have made a further point namely, that not only are the children in England younger on entry to primary school, but also have a greater awareness of concepts of print, where the baseline for this is not entry to school. This I would argue is an erroneous conclusion from this data.

Attitude to various aspects of schooling

In the report there is a chapter devoted to school climate based on responses to the questionnaires by head teachers and by pupils. Scotland is one of the countries singled out for mention because more than 60 per cent of students attended schools perceived by the head teachers as having high morale, high academic expectations, regard for school property and a high level of parental support (Mullis *et al:* 242). In Scotland and Sweden a very positive response is given with regard to school resources; and absenteeism is not regarded as a problem.

When studying this section of the report I observed that there were no entries in the tables for England either from head teachers or pupils; nor is an explanation given for this either in the International or the NFER report. I therefore raised this with NFER and was told that these questions were omitted from the questionnaires in England.

The items were subject to the normal review process during the preparation of the materials for use in England. These particular items were withdrawn at the request of DfES because it was felt that these areas required more sophisticated data collection methods than were being proposed. (correspondence with L. Twist of NFER).

It is interesting to speculate what the responses would have been in England. This could have been significant particularly since, in spite of the high achievement, the pupils' attitude to reading and self confidence in their reading was surprisingly low.

Conclusions

As may be apparent it took some detective work to tease out these points from this study, and there may be others, had I probed further. There was careful monitoring of the sampling and the scoring. New tests were devised for the study. It contains a great deal of interesting data. However, surely the points raised here with regard to the findings, and, for only selected countries indicate the need for caution in interpreting any international study, even one as carefully monitored as this. It is perhaps appropriate to finish by drawing attention to a few specific findings:

A sex difference in attainment in favour of girls was found in all countries. Girls were also more likely to read for pleasure at home; however, the difference was not apparent with reading for information. In England the gulf was greatest between boys and girls in the weakest group.

In the following respects results for England differed from those of other countries, in spite of its high average level of attainment:

- England is reported to be one of the countries with the widest span of attainment.
- The range of reading ability in rural and urban schools, and in schools with the highest proportions of economically disadvantaged pupils is wider in England than in most other countries.
- Ten-year-old pupils in England have a poorer attitude towards reading, and read less often for fun than pupils of the same age in other countries.

These and many other points in the report have relevance for the approach to the teaching of reading, the nature of the materials used with the children and the likelihood that the children will retain an interest in reading for a variety of purposes.

On claims such as the following the jury must remain out!

- Children in England start school earlier, show more reading readiness and have a higher level of early learning skills than their international peers (Twist *et al*, 2003a: 60)
- The relative support for literacy activities in the homes of children in England is greater than that enjoyed by their counterparts in other countries.

Footnote in 2014: It seems likely that there would be similar anomalies in some aspects of sampling in other international studies where between countries attainment is assessed. Yet we still find extravagant claims made either of delight, or concern at lowering of standards, or a fall in place in the league tables. Blame is then attributed by politicians to either a particular political party or some method of teaching reading. The politicians then look with envy at particular countries that have scored high, and on occasion draw dangerous or simplistic conclusions.

One must suspect that if a similar analysis were undertaken on the recently published Programme for International Assessment Student Assessment (PISA) some anomalies might well be uncovered. For that study half a million 15-year-olds in 64 countries and territories were tested (see *Education Journal,* December, 2013 for a series of articles on the results of PISA).

References

Mullis, I. V. S., Martin, M. O, Gonzalez, E. J and Kennedy, A. M. (2003) *PIRLS 2001 International Report: IEA`s study of reading literacy achievement in primary schools.* Chestnut Hill, M.A: Boston College. Download from http://isc.bc.edu/pirls2001i/PIRLS2001_Pubs_IR.html

Twist, L., Sainsbury, M., Woodthorpe, A and Whetton, C. (2003a) *PIRLS Progress in International Literacy Study, National Report for England: reading all over the world.* Slough: NFER.

Twist, L., Sainsbury, M., Woodthorpe, A and Whetton, C. (2003b) `New Evidence on Reading Standards`. *Education Journal* Issue 69: 28-31.

Chapter 20
Literacies in and for a Changing World: what is the evidence?

This chapter is a shortened and edited version of chapter 5 in *Improving the Quality of Childhood in Europe,* 2012, vol 3, C. Clouder, B. Heys, M. Matthes and P. Sullivan (eds), based on a paper given in Brussels in 2011.

Outline

Even in the most advanced societies there are still adults, including young adults who have recently left school, whose literacy competence is not adequate to meet the demands of life and work in an increasingly digitalised world. Many make every attempt to hide their inadequacy. Successful adult literacy programmes are one way of breaking the cycle of intergenerational illiteracy, as the children most likely to fail are those from families where the parents' literacy level is low. Evidence is now available that processing and understanding written language for a variety of purposes is a complex process and that no one simple method meets the needs of all children, or all languages. There are additional problems in learning to read in a language where the sound to symbol relationship is less regular. In countries where the formal teaching of reading starts at an earlier age the standard of literacy is not higher; this may also lead to a negative attitude to reading, particularly among boys. Successful schools and adult literacy programmes have a number of things in common: early intervention with sound diagnostic procedures; well trained teachers using imaginative curricula; inclusion of the new technologies; high expectations.

In this chapter brief reference will be made to implications from several of my own researches; studies of preschool children; and a study of pupils in the first year of secondary school. In the secondary school research the literacy demands made by the subject teachers and the pupils' response within different subject areas were studied. The attitudes of the various subject departments to the literacy needs of their subjects were also investigated. The remainder of the chapter is devoted to evidence from selected researches and official reports as to how functional literacy is currently being defined; what has so far been achieved; who has been left behind. The role of families, schools and the community will be considered. Finally I will consider how and when we can identify and assist those with difficulties, both children and adults. The annotated reference list at the end of the chapter will enable readers to find further information.

Introduction

This is a written version of a paper delivered in Brussels in 2011, and while the message is the same, the distinction between these two modes of communication, spoken and written, is important. For many years emphasis was placed on the similarities between spoken and written language, almost as if printed language was merely speech written down, a visual representation of speech rather than a language communication in a different medium to an unknown person. Coupled with this assumption was the idea that only teachers of younger children, and those working with older backward readers, need expertise in literacy. Over the years there have been claims for one or other method as the method for teaching all beginner readers. In some instances, and in the hands of the initial enthusiasts, there may have been a dramatic rise in standards with the introduction of a new method. Evidence is against such a simple solution, or that one approach meets the needs of all children, or all languages. There is now a greater appreciation of the cognitive processing involved in comprehension of written language for different purposes. A sound foundation in spoken language is an important prerequisite for learning to read. Stories read, and reread to children, coupled with dialogue around the story with the mother, father or other adult, provide a valuable foundation for young children, extending their vocabulary, helping them to appreciate the forms and features of written language, and not least to enjoy its variety and richness.

Furthermore, there is no evidence that school systems that rush to introduce the formal teaching of reading at an earlier and earlier age achieve higher levels of literacy among the adult population. Formal reading programmes introduced at an early age may result in negative attitudes towards reading in some of the children, particularly boys, who may seldom read and thus do not maintain even their limited literacy skills into adulthood.

The comprehension of narrative prose, extraction of information from textbooks, understanding of written instructions and digital literacy all require very different skills. Children's initial experiences of written language should be comprehensive, stimulating and meaningful to them. Thus all teachers in primary schools and subject teachers in secondary schools, have a part to play in partnership with each other and with parents. There is evidence of intergenerational illiteracy, that where parents cannot read they are likely to have children with limited literacy. In some instances this may be a self-fulfilling prophecy, where professionals have too limited aspirations for some pupils that may lead to lowered expectations, even a more limited curriculum for some groups of pupils. Successful schools, those where there is a stimulating curriculum, good leadership, partnership between professionals and with parents, high expectations of all pupils, clear diagnostic procedures followed by early intervention, can enable virtually all pupils to become literate. The involvement of parents in intervention programmes, even those with limited literacy themselves, has been shown to have the greatest success. Furthermore the parents may also be stimulated to become 'functionally literate', breaking cycles of deprivation, and enabling them to achieve longer term employment and a richer cultural life for themselves (see 'When mama can't read: counteracting intergenerational illiteracy', Cooter, 2006).

Pupils in secondary schools who are described as illiterate are unlikely to be completely unable to read; rather they have such a low level of competence that they are unlikely to read for pleasure or to understand the complex meanings in various forms of written language. As adults they will avoid situations requiring them to read, and their level of literacy will become lower rather than be maintained. Many adults with limited literacy make every attempt to hide this; thus, even where support programmes are available there may be problems in identifying those adults who need support.

There is a reciprocal relationship between reading and writing, each helping to develop the other. It is simplistic to assume a sequential development from oral to silent reading and from reading to writing, or that children should only be encouraged to write when they have acquired a certain level of reading fluency. Many with limited competence in reading think they are more competent than is the case, and have a negative attitude to books and other printed materials. They are thus unlikely to broaden their knowledge of written language. As a consequence when required to write they produce writing that fails to communicate, or is little more than colloquial speech written down, a far cry from the richness of real written language. (See *Awakening to Literacy,* Goelman, Oberg and Smith, 1984 and *New Directions in the Study of Reading,* Clark, 1985)

Selected researches by the author with continuing relevance

My interest in literacy and child development was stimulated early in my career when as a primary school teacher I was responsible for a class of 54 children aged 7-8 years of age who had started school at five years of age. As I became aware of a number of issues with policy implications I was able to secure funding to investigate these with a wide range of children from preschool to secondary age, children who were advanced in their literacy development and others who were struggling in learning to read and write. I realise that there are still lessons to be learnt from these researches. I therefore gave a brief outline of a selection of these in my lecture in Brussels. Here I will discuss only two, those of pre-school children and pupils in secondary schools. I have omitted my studies of children with reading difficulties and into children who were already reading fluently when they started school as these are discussed in chapters 4 and 5.

Preschool studies

The focus of one of a series of observational studies of children aged three and four in nursery schools was on children who had high or low interest in books and stories. We were able to show the influence of their homes and also the effect of stories on their appreciation of written language (see chapter 8 here and Lomax in Clark and Cheyne, 1979, chapter 6). In another study, also as early as the 1970s, parents who would have been labelled `disadvantaged` were supported as they interacted with their young preschool children around books and discussed these experiences with other parents. Not only were the parents` expectations and self-confidence raised, but also the children`s first teachers, who had interacted with the parents in advance of the children entering school, were more positive in their expectations of the parents and children (Donachy in Clark and Cheyne, 1979, Section III). A recent study of three and four-year-old children showed how competent with a variety of technologies are many of today`s children even before they enter school. It is debatable whether teachers take sufficient advantage of this in planning their curriculum for young children (Stephen, McPake and Plowman in Clark and Tucker, 2010).

Pupils with learning difficulties in secondary schools

The focus of this research was 12 year-old pupils in their first year in seven secondary schools in Scotland. A new policy for helping pupils with difficulties was being introduced in these schools where all first year classes were of `mixed ability`. Sixty-three target pupils were observed in a number of classrooms. They were nominated by subject teachers, three within a class, one nominated by all subject teachers as good, one as poor, one whose performance fluctuated from subject to subject. Samples of their written work were analysed and writing tasks were set involving three different types of communication: narrative writing, a science report following a video presentation and a description for a younger child of how to play a game of their choice. The views of promoted/senior staff and subject teachers were sought on the level of competence in literacy required for their subject and whether they felt any responsibility for identifying and supporting those with limited literacy. We found that in its early stages this initiative was still fragile, dependent on the continuing presence of a few key individuals. We were disturbed at the lack of support for the pupils with difficulties, many of whom were not sufficiently competent to benefit from the formal curriculum and type of assessment expected of them. Even the spelling level of some was still too low for them to communicate in writing. It was therefore a matter of great concern that many subject teachers, including English teachers, did not regard it as one of their responsibilities to improve the literacy level of the least competent, or make allowance for their deficits.

This research dates from 1980s (Clark, Barr and McKee, 1982). However, evidence from a recent research in 11 countries on *Teaching Struggling Adolescent Readers* (ADORE, 2010) suggests that there is still a long way to go in developing whole school policies that provide those with difficulties with both a stimulating curriculum and support to enable them to overcome their difficulties.

What has been achieved?

Literacy levels in schools

Evidence from a variety of sources on literacy (narrative and informational) in schools has raised concern in many European countries, including the United Kingdom. Two main sources are the IEA PIRLS study in 2001 of 10-year-olds in 35 countries who will now be reaching adulthood and the more recent OECD PISA study in 2009 of 15-year-olds in 65 countries (24 members of EU) where not only levels of achievement but attitudes to literacy and school factors were explored. Many governments are disturbed at their ranking and whether they are retaining their place in league tables. What is also of concern is that in most countries there are many children who leave school with very limited literacy skills and also with no desire to engage in any literacy activities or to improve their level. Their failure has adverse consequences for their employability, their family and social life. In all countries the level of literacy in boys seems to be lower than that of girls, and many boys have negative attitudes to books. Some ethnic groups and socially disadvantaged groups also have low literacy levels. If pupils reach adulthood without becoming functionally literate there are likely to be problems in identifying them to provide them with the necessary support, as many deny they have problems, or do all they can to hide their illiteracy. Successful schools can achieve literacy for most if not all their pupils. One study in England by Ofsted (the inspection body for England) considered what features appeared to be crucial in the schools and other institutions inspected, particularly for those at risk (*Removing Barriers to Literacy,* Ofsted, 2011). The following were stressed: the importance of an emphasis on speaking and listening skills from an early age; teachers with high expectations; carefully planned provision to meet individual needs with early diagnosis and early intervention for those with problems; literacy training for all staff and partnership with parents.

Raising literacy levels in adults

Historically, there has been a deep distrust of literacy, and possibly still is in some cultures, or for some people. Limited access to everyday contact with written language and a lack of access to other readers and writers who might support literate competence creates a complex obstacle to literacy (Whitescarver and Kalman, 2009). Yet there is a link between adult learning and civic activities such as voting, and those with the poorest literacy skills often lead an isolated life. It should be remembered that marginalized communities may use reading and writing for a variety of purposes that are unacknowledged by mainstream institutions, and some may have a sophisticated oral tradition. *Literacy in the Information Age* (OECD, 2000) is a valuable source of information. The data was collected between 1994-98, from a nationally representative sample in 20 countries (age group 16-65). Three aspects of literacy and at several levels of functioning were assessed: prose literacy; document literacy and quantitative literacy. There was a wide variation between countries in the extent of inequality in the population distribution of literacy skills; countries with the highest levels had been most successful in bolstering the literacy levels of their least advantaged. Initial education was the main factor in improving the literacy levels, particularly of youth from lower socio-economic backgrounds (89). Even in the most economically advanced societies a `literacy deficit` was reported, with many adults without a suitable minimum skill to cope with the demands of modern life and work. The following points are stressed in the report:

- The importance of growing up in a literate culture and of high expectations in schools;

- gender differences are noted as in other reports;
- the need for regular engagement in reading activities to maintain skills.
- it was felt that special measures were required to assist adults.

A recent report by the Inspectorate for Scotland, *Improving Adult Literacy in Scotland* (HMIE, 2010) assesses the extent to which adult literacy programmes in colleges, local authorities and in prisons in Scotland meet the needs of the adult learners. Successful programmes were found to involve good planning, partnerships, assessment of needs and monitoring of progress, together with effective use of ICT.

The National Institute of Adult and Continuing Education (NIACE) established an Enquiry into Adult Literacy in England; lifelong literacy, in, out and beyond work. The scope of this enquiry was to ascertain: what are the challenges; what has worked well; what has not worked well and what are the priorities for the future. The final report published in 2011 stresses the importance of breaking the cycle of inter-generational difficulties with literacy. More teachers must be trained and there need to be more innovative and cross-sector partnerships to help the many millions of adults who do not have the literacy skills they need for everyday life in the modern world.

The level of literacy among many pupils when they leave statutory education may be higher than in the past, but some pupils and particular groups in EU countries, still leave school without the competence to enable them to function in an advanced society, particularly as the literacy demands increase. In the current economic climate there are high levels of unemployment among the younger adults who have not yet been employed; many of these will still only have limited literacy skills. In the United Kingdom, for example, in the age group 16-19, the group referred to as NEETs (Not in education, employment or training), has increased over the past ten years and was claimed in 2011 to be one in eight of the age group. This is one of the groups where further literacy education is important, yet they are a neglected group. (www.poverty.org.uk).

The languages of literacy

There is surprisingly little research information on the difference in complexity in learning to read in languages where there is a more or less regular relationship between the sounds and spelling of words, or of learning to read in a language that is not your first language. Yet, it is increasingly common for children to learn to read in more than one language, and is estimated that currently at least half the world's children learn to read in their second language (Deacon and Cain, 2011).There must now be many classrooms in the EU with numerous different languages spoken by the children, not necessarily understood by their classmates, or even the professionals. One comparative intervention study using Reading Recovery diagnostic procedures followed by one-to-one individual support for young at risk children was undertaken by Hobsbaum (2003). This study involved five countries with different starting dates for children entering primary school, namely England, Ireland, Denmark, Spain and Slovakia, countries with languages of different levels of regularity in their orthography. The six subtests in Reading Recovery diagnosis, a programme developed by Marie Clay in New Zealand in 1980s provided sensitive measures for assessing the children's strengths and weaknesses as a guide to the most appropriate strategies to help them to make progress. This has been widely used in many countries and was recommended following sponsored funded research in England with government support. There is a European Centre co-ordinating this work based in The Institute of Education in London University (www.ioe.ac.uk or www.everychildareader.org.uk). See chapter 7.

In a further research entitled 'Foundation literacy acquisition in European orthographies,' Seymour, Aro and Erskine (2003) studied the foundations of literacy in a number of European countries with more or less regular spelling. This revealed that in the majority of European countries children became accurate and fluent at the foundation level before the end of their first school year. The exceptions were those learning to read in Portuguese, Danish, and particularly in English. These findings did not appear to be related to the age of starting school. Hanley (2010) claims that a number of studies have shown that word recognition skills in children learning to read English develop more slowly than other countries using alphabetic systems. He compared the word recognition skills of matched groups of children learning to read in Welsh (with a transparent orthography) and children learning to read in English (with an opaque orthography). He found a `tail` of poor English readers, but no such tail of those learning to read in Welsh. He argues that English is a difficult writing system for children to learn.

The PROREAD study (2009) was undertaken in six EU countries with test data from 3,000 children and 6,500 remedial teachers to investigate the effectiveness of remedial support for poor readers. It is argued that for poor reader support to be successful it should be aimed at students and teachers. This is one of the few reports where the influence of learning to read in different languages is considered. It is argued that learning to read in different languages does not require different cognitive skills and thus evidence of effective intervention programmes across language barriers may be valuable.

The way ahead

There have been intervention programmes that have raised the literacy level of most young children. These have been successful where they have had a coherent policy for reading tuition covering the whole area, with all schools participating, additional training for staff and extra resources.

The following are the most important issues that require to be addressed if the levels of literacy in the European countries are to meet the needs of adults in the twenty-first century:

- Speaking and listening as a foundation for literacy development must be recognised;
- the changing nature of literacy, including the impact of new technologies for children as well as adults, must be acknowledged, including their value as a new medium of instruction, and as requiring new strategies from readers and writers;

- the differential problems of learning to read in more or less orthographically regular languages should be acknowledged;
- the characteristics of successful schools and school systems must be analysed, those that result not only in high average standards of literacy, but also avoid a long tail of very poor readers;
- pre-service training and continuing development of teachers must be planned that will provide them with a range of strategies and insights giving them high expectations for all their pupils, with a creative curriculum that will motivate the development for a variety of purposes;
- the importance of a partnership with parents must be acknowledged, including those whose own literacy level is limited, to encourage their participation and to motivate them to improve their own literacy;
- the importance of identifying assessment measures that both monitor progress within and between schools and provide diagnosis of difficulties for those at risk leading to early intervention;
- the need to identify and support adults whose literacy level is so limited that it reduces their prospects of continuous employment or restricts their participation in the social and cultural life of their community.

In February 2011 the European Commission set up an independent group of experts from 11 countries to meet over the following eighteen months to assess how to raise literacy levels, to analyse scientific evidence and evaluate what policies work best. The report was published in 2012 (EU high level group of experts on literacy; final report). The following are among the recommendations:

- Adopt a coherent literacy curriculum;
- create the role of specialist teachers of reading as resource persons for other primary and secondary teachers.

To quote:

> Ensure that all newly qualified teachers obtain a master's degree, with competences in, for example, critical evaluation of literacy research and new instructional methods, tailoring instruction to student language diversity and engaging parents in their children's reading and writing work at school.

Note: A special issue of *Literacy,* a journal of the United Kingdom Literacy Association, published in November 2011, was devoted to Literacy and Politics with articles from England, Scotland and New Zealand covering many of the topics discussed in this chapter. In England, concern is expressed at the lack of attention to the expertise of practitioners in policy debates and explanations for the gender gap in literacy attainment are considered. The implications for literacy teaching of the increasing cultural and linguistic diversity in New Zealand, as in many other countries is considered also what changes are required in the early years curriculum to counteract New Zealand's failure in recent years to maintain its high ranking in international surveys. Resisting deficit approaches to learning in adult literacy practices in Scotland is the focus for another article. The journal which has valuable reference lists on these topics can be accessed online (www.wileyolinelibrary.com).

Annotated references

Clark, M. M. and Cheyne, W. M. eds (1979) *Studies in Preschool Education.* Edinburgh: Hodder and Stoughton. This reports a number of researches in newly opened nursery schools and a parental programme for disadvantaged families (see C. Lomax and W. Donachy).

Clark, M. M, Barr, J and McKee, F (1982). *Pupils with Learning Difficulties in the Secondary School.* Birmingham: University of Birmingham. Report of research undertaken in seven secondary schools in Scotland 1980-1.The aim was to investigate a developing policy for support within secondary schools for pupils in their first year with learning difficulties.

Clark, M. M. (1985) (ed) *New Directions in the Study of Reading*. Lewes: Falmer Press. Sections on Oral and written language; Readiness and the language of reading; Reading and writing, reciprocal relationships.

Clark, M. M. (1994) *Young Literacy Learners: how we can help them*. Leamington Spa: Scholastic. There are illustrations of young children's understanding of written language.

Clark, M. M. and Tucker, S (eds) (2010) *Early Childhoods in a Changing World*. Stoke on Trent: Trentham. There are case studies from around the world. See chapter 14, 'Digital Technologies in the Home: the experience of 3- and 4-year-olds in Scotland' (C. Stephen, J. McPake and L. Plowman).

Cooter, K. S. (2006) 'When mama can't read: counteracting intergenerational illiteracy'. *The Reading Teacher*. 59 (7): 698-702.

Deacon, H. and Cain. K. (2011) 'What have we learnt from learning to read in more than one language'. *Journal of Research in Reading,* 34 (1): 1-5. This is a special issue on learning to read in more than one language.

Hanley, J. R. (2010) 'English is a difficult writing system for children to learn: evidence from children learning to read in Wales'. In *Interdisciplinary Perspectives on Learning to Read* (eds) K. Hall, U. Goswami, S. Ellis and J. Soler. London: Routledge.

Hobsbaum, A. (2003) 'Assessing early literacy – in five languages'. *Literacy Today*. 37 see www.nationalliteracytrust.net.

Seymour, P. H .K., Aro, M. and Erskine, J. M. (2003) 'Foundation literacy acquisition in European orthographies'. *British Journal of Psychology*. 94: 143-174.

Whitescarver, K. and Kalman, J. (2009) 'Extending traditional explanations of illiteracy: historical and cross-cultural perspectives'. *Compare*. 39 (4): 497-511.

Selection of official reports:

ADORE (2010) *Teaching Struggling Adolescent Readers.* www.adore-project.eu.

HMIE (2010) *Improving Adult Literacy in Scotland.* This is an evaluation of Adult Literacy Provision delivered by Colleges, Local Authority, Community Learning and Development Services and Prisons. www.scotland.gov.uk and www.hmie.gov.uk. Assesses the extent to which the provision matches the diverse needs. Also see Outline of Scottish Government`s Vision for Literacies. NB HMIE is Her Majesty`s Inspectorate of Education for Scotland (not Ofsted).

IEA (2003) *Progress in International Reading Literacy Study (PIRLS)* undertaken in 2001 reported in 2003.Ten-year-olds in 35 countries. www.pirls.org/pirls2001, with a separate report for England .(www.nfer.ac.uk). Also see chapter 19 in this book, `International Studies of reading such as PIRLS - a cautionary tale`. Further information in PIRLS 2006 was published in 2007, a report from 40 countries. Assessment of literacy was in two parts literary and information.

National Literacy Trust (2010) *Literacy: State of the Nation: A picture of literacy in UK today.* www.literacytrust.org.uk. This report has reference list of official documents for UK.

NIACE (2011) *Enquiry into Adult Literacy in England: Lifelong Literacy, In, Out and Beyond Work* Enquiry commenced 2010 ten years after previous report. Progress Report December 2010. Scope of the Commission to ascertain: What are the challenges, what has worked well; what has not worked well and priorities for the future. NIACE: National Institute of Adult and Continuing Education.

OECD (2000) *Literacy in the Information Age: Final Report of the International Adult Literacy Survey.* www.oecd.org.

OECD (2010) *Programme for International Student Assessment (PISA)* Reading, Maths and Science every three years since 2000, 2009 main focus on literacy. Fifteen-year-olds in 65 countries (separate reports for England www.nfer.ac.uk and Scotland www.scotland.gov.uk). Girls do better than boys, importance of parental involvement, need for autonomy of schools within a well-controlled overall framework, attendance at pre-school, in less selective systems those from lower socio-economic classes do better. See also article by Andreas Schleicher of OECD presented in January 2010, `The Quality of Childhood: Evidence from the Programme for International Student Assessment (PISA)`. Two further linked studies `Against the odds – disadvantaged students who succeed in school` and `Quality time for students learning in and out of school`. *Literacy Skills for the World of Tomorrow.* A further PISA report has appeared in 2013, See *Education Journal,* Issue 184 for reviews of the findings.

Ofsted (2011) *Removing Barriers to Literacy* www.ofsted,gov.uk. Ofsted Inspection of preschools, primary and secondary schools, colleges, independent providers, LEAs, prison and young offenders` provision in England during 2008-10 to identify successful settings, particularly for .those at risk.

PROREAD Bromert, L. (2009) *Cognitive and Educational Profiling of Reading and Poor Reader Support within the EU.*
www.ec.europa.eu/education.

NB. The Report of the European Working Party EU High Level Group of Experts on Literacy: Final Report 2012 can be downloaded from www.ec.europa.eu/education/literacy/resources/finalreport.

Chapter 21
Insights on Literacy from Research

Introduction

This final chapter brings together insights on the development of written language from a number of sources, including my own studies. I have drawn on some publications cited elsewhere in the book; others have been introduced here to widen the discussion. The illustrative examples reveal ways in which children's development parallels some aspects of the history of written languages. My aim throughout the book has been to show that knowledge of research on literacy is relevant to professionals, those involved in policy decisions, and practitioners. Their sensitivity to the stage of development and needs of individual children and adults can be enhanced by insights from literacy research.

The development of written language

People have tried to record words in some form throughout history; amazingly varied ways have been used for written communication. Some representations are closer to what we regard as drawing, with a direct association between the features of the object and the written representation. Written communication may take a variety of forms within different cultures and has changed greatly over the years. There may be differences in the way shapes follow each other on the page in written language, from left to right, from right to left, from top to bottom, or alternating (Balmuth, 1982).

The use of spaces to represent meaningful groups of sounds is a convention we adopt in some written languages. Those of us who can read tend to believe that speech also is in the form of words, with a pause representing word boundaries. There are no such gaps in the flow of speech; this may be one reason that we find it difficult to grasp the flow of meaning in speech in a language with which we are not familiar. We may not have sufficient awareness of the probabilities of particular structures within words, word endings and sequences of words, in languages with which we are unfamiliar, to enable us to split the flow of sounds into meaningful units.

It is a convention in alphabetic languages that there is a relationship between the approximate length of a written word and the time it takes to say it. The relationship between sound and symbol might have been otherwise, and is so in non-alphabetic languages. In *The Roots of Phonics: a historical introduction* (Balmuth, 1982) Balmuth traces the history of writing systems in general, and the English writing system, spoken English and English spelling patterns. In *The Psychology of Reading*, Kennedy gives a brief history of the development of writing systems, with interesting illustrations from different cultures and through the ages. (Kennedy, 1984)

We take silent reading for granted, but it was not common practice initially, as may be seen from a fourth century example recorded by St Augustine. To quote from *Women who Read are Dangerous* (translated from Bollmann, S 2008: 26):

> On his (usually unannounced) visits to the bishop, he would find him "silently immersed in reading" for Ambrose never read aloud… his voice was silent, and his tongue was at rest….Does he wish not to be distracted during these brief moments, Augustine asks, or not to have to enter into discussions with other listeners?

In this same publication, in the Foreword, Karen Joy Fowler, traces the history of reactions to women reading, other than when associated with piety and chastity. The book is graphically illustrated with famous paintings over the ages of women in the act of reading.

Features of written English

To any literate adult the relationship between oral and written language may seem obvious. What else could the letters represent except the sounds of speech? What else could the series of letters with blanks in between represent except the words we speak? However, young children and illiterate adults may not appreciate this and may be interpreting the writing they see in consistent but erroneous ways. They may not appreciate the functions of letters, words, numbers and punctuation. The language of our instruction may add to this confusion. Most young children have indeed come across the word `letter` before they come to school, however, some may only have heard it used as a message received through the post as opposed to an alphabetic symbol. See chapter 8 for illustrations of young children's growing awareness of the conventions of drawing and writing, and the wide variation in children of the same age.

A study of the development of our alphabetic writing system is helpful in gaining insight into some of the early assumptions of young children as they come to grips with the conventions of written language. Their individual development may mirror in some aspects that development. It is interesting to note, for example, that lower case letters were a later development than capital letters and that early alphabetic writing did not have spaces between words. I have illustrations from children adopting both these strategies. Examples of the early attempts at spelling by the young fluent readers in my study in 1970s, revealed even when words were correctly spelt there might be a mixture of upper and lower case letters. (see chapter 5). For example:

BeG friEnd lOuD womeN

Glenda Bissex's study of her young son's early written communications, before he started school, reported in GNYS AT WRK, (1980) were mentioned in several chapters in Section I. As she traces his development, she describes how Paul, at the age of 5:2, and not yet at school, presented her with the following typed message:

EFUKANOPNKAZIWILGEVUAKANOPENR

In her bewilderment she asked him to read it aloud to her which he did as:

`If you can open cans, I will give you a can opener`.

As he read it, he pointed to the appropriate letters and paused between words. Had she not then mentioned that many writers put spaces between words he might not have so soon appreciated this feature of written English which he then adopted. (Bissex, 1980: 11) Glenda Bissex gives as her first example of Paul's written messages at the age of five, his attempt to attract her attention in a new way. He printed:

RUDF

For the next month Paul wrote avidly, developing an alphabetic spelling system that served his needs, and producing a variety of forms (signs, captions, notes, statements, lists, directions, a game, and a story'. (Bissex, 1980: 3)

Bissex does provide us with the meaning of these words: `Are you deaf?` In 1980 when I first read her book, I did not single this example out as possibly an early example of texting; this thought only occurred to me when checking the quotation recently.

I have examples of writing from a teen age boy with language difficulties whose problems with spelling were not merely that words were spelt incorrectly but his ideas of word boundaries were faulty; thus a dictionary would have been of limited help to him. The following is an extract from an essay he wrote for me, showing the unfortunate effect of his limited grasp of spelling conventions and word boundaries on what was a reasonably competent argument:

Can yoos you to theyr best edvanteg and then made shoore that you bont get the....taking infor manhen from you .....that has been carfuly colected for the yoos of your self.at that meeting....then has to be handes over to somdodya ells to yoos.

When children come to learn to read, they have to learn to observe new features in order to discriminate letters of the alphabet and words. In addition they have to understand the language used to describe letters, numbers, words and punctuation. Are children clear about the distinction between `three` and 3, both representing a number? Ask adults to define `word`, and some will refer to a group of letters. Yet, some words have only one letter, such as A and I, confusing for any child who has come to think that a word is a group of letters! See the comment of The Red Queen to Alice, quoted at the end of chapter 8:

> `Of course you know your A B C`, said the Red Queen....`I can even read words of one letter`... `You`ll come to that in time`.

Pre-school children would have come to accept that something does not change its name, or become a different object whichever way it faces. Capital letters are more distinctive than lower case letters, and most retain their identity even when reversed, in contrast to lower case letters. I observed in some of my young fluent readers a preference for using capital letters, at least in place of some lower case letters. Perhaps this was because they are easier to identify when your motor co-ordination is not well-developed. We should not be surprised that young children make mistakes, and that a number of these are reversals; rather we should be impressed at how quickly they come to recognise the critical features of written language.

In my community study of children with reading difficulties, 1544 children were assessed individually on a word reading test at the age of seven. More boys than girls were backward in learning to read at that age. The children's laterality preferences were also tested, and it should be noted that there was no relationship between reading level and either left-handedness, crossed laterality (of hand and eye preference) or doubtful handedness. However, more boys than girls were left-handed. Furthermore at that age, 60 per cent of the children still found it difficult to differentiate right and left. These were important findings at that time in view of the controversy on dyslexia, and relationships claimed, based on small samples of clinic cases (Clark, 1970). The results of the spelling test are also relevant. This was taken by 230 of these children at the age of eight, the fifteen per cent with the lowest scores on the word reading test. An analysis of their reversals was made to ascertain how common this still was in backward readers at that age. Reversed and inverted letters, and reversals of letters within a word, were counted. Such features were found in about half this group of backward readers, and the reversals were commoner in those with the lowest reading ages. Thus, when seeing young children in a clinic whose reading level is low, such reversals are likely to be the rule rather than the exception.

Such problems are not confined to young children, as can be seen from the following extract from a message sent to me by a well-educated dyslexic adult, who even in his twenties interspersed lower and upper case letters:

> I must ApolAgise for Being so lat. I Don't normaly wer a watch ..I only Discovred This LATAR....

This young man had learnt to read successfully, but only at about twelve years of age. Until then his experience of written language had been orally presented to enable him to experience a wide curriculum. Later, with the aid of a scribe, he had achieved a university degree, yet as can be seen, he was only at a rudimentary stage in written communication. Indeed it must have taken courage for him to send this message to me, to explain why he missed our first meeting. He came to make a presentation to my students who were training to become educational psychologists, and was articulate in the way he was able to explain to them the range of his problems, and to distinguish spoken and written language. He informed us that he insisted that the examination answers he dictated should be transcribed, as they were written language, intended to be read rather than heard.

Charles Read in *Children's Creative Spelling* (1986) analyses the types of representations of words to be found in children's early attempts at writing. In my research on Young Fluent Readers, discussed in chapter 5, I showed that these children were already becoming sensitized to English spelling patterns and that most knew whether or not they could spell words correctly. In contrast, I found that some older children and adults with spelling problems with whom I worked, not only found it difficult to decide whether they had spelt a word wrongly, they were not even confident when they had spelt a word correctly. In order to assess the extent of their difficulties, an initial task I set them was to write an essay for me, using as wide a language as possible, not worrying if they couldn't spell the words. I then asked them to underline any words they thought were incorrectly spelt and put question marks at those about which they were doubtful. Only then were the full stresses they faced revealed to them and to me. Many underlined as wrongly spelt words that were correct; it must have been very difficult in these circumstances to concentrate on what they were writing, particularly when a high premium was placed on correct spelling.

In our research in secondary schools, discussed in chapter 20, we set the first year pupils, aged about twelve years of age, three types of writing task in addition to a spelling test. These were a science report, a description for a younger child of how to play a game of their choice and an essay with the title, `From fear to safety`. We were able to show how strongly the demands of the task influenced the apparent spelling competence and breadth of language used by these pupils. We were also able to show the range of competence within a single age-group, not always appreciated by the subject specialists. Some pupils were clearly not able to fulfil many of the written tasks with which they were confronted. (Clark, Barr and McKee, 1982) Similar evidence was collected by Jennifer Barr who worked with me during her PhD on spelling. A very useful summary of her research was published in 1985 as *Understanding Children Spelling*. She found that the spelling of one boy whom she helped appeared to his teacher to have deteriorated until the written work was analysed. He was having the courage to risk take and use a wider vocabulary; his spelling had in fact improved.

Margaret Peters was responsible for pioneering research into child and teacher variables which influence children`s spelling progress. *In Spelling: caught or taught?* Peters (1967 and new edition 1985) indicates practical implications from her work; full details of which are given *in Success in Spelling* (Peters, 1970). She contrasts the task of reading with that of accurate spelling. While flying saucer would be read accurately by most eight-year-olds out of context, in her study of 967 ten-year-olds, fewer than half wrote it correctly, the remainder between them offered around 200 alternative spellings. The commonest were sauser, sorcer, sacer (Peters, 1970: 95). However, many of the errors were such that a dictionary would not have helped the children to find the correct spelling! She stresses, however, that spelling is a skill that can be taught to and learned by most children. We found a similar range of spelling errors in pupils in their first year in secondary school. (Clark, Barr and McKee, 1982)

Spell it Out: the singular story of English spelling by David Crystal (2012) is a more recent valuable source on the development of written English. He stresses that literacy involves three skills, not two; reading, writing and spelling. He traces the development in English towards the convention of a correct spelling for words, claiming that many of the features of English spelling were shaped because they were recommended by individual writers. Dr Johnston, he claims, did for British spelling what Webster did for American English (196). Spelling, he claims, is a matter of internalising letter sequences in words, and the more opportunities children have to see these sequences the better. He reminds us that currently many people's names are still pronounced differently by different people.

Crystal provides an interesting illustration of the complexity of English spelling, and why spell checkers are of only limited value in identifying errors in written English. He quotes the first two stanzas of an ode to a spell checker, by Mark Eckman and Jerrold H. Zar (from Crystal, 2012:7):

> I have a spelling checker,
> It came with my PC.
> It plane lee marks four my revue
> Miss steaks aye can knot sea.
>
> Eye ran this poem threw it,
> Your sure reel glad two no.
> Its vary polished in it's weigh.
> My checker tolled me sew.

A spell checker would not spot anything wrong here, yet count how many words are indeed incorrectly spelt!

Lewis Carroll's famous books for children first published over a hundred years ago are wonderful source books for insights into the subtleties of written forms of the English language and the fun to be derived from play with words (Carroll, 1865 and 1872). Several examples are given at the end of chapters 8 and 10.

Orthographies and Literacy

A valuable source of information on the impact of different orthographies on learning to be literate is the *Handbook of Orthography and Literacy* (Malatesha Joshi and Aaron, 2013). In Section I there are 26 chapters giving a wide ranging account of literacy acquisition in different writing systems; Section II describes literacy acquisition from cross-linguistic perspectives; Section III develops the theme of literacy acquisition: instructional perspectives. Two chapters are particularly relevant to the present discussion, chapter 27, `The theoretic framework for beginning reading in different orthographies` is by Seymour whose earlier publication was mentioned in chapter 20. (Seymour, Aro and Erskine 2003)

Seymour points out that:

> Languages differ in their phonological and morphological structures, and these aspects may influence the way in which literacy is acquired. Equally, the languages have different writing systems (orthographies) that vary in the way in which speech and meaning are represented and, indeed in the consistency and logic of the relationship. (Seymour, 2013: 441-442)

He cites Chinese and Japanese, Hebrew and Arabic in one group, and alphabetic scripts in which the letters represent the vowel and consonant phonemes in another. These latter he divides into shallow orthographies in which the relationship is coherent and consistent (such as Finnish) and deep orthographies `in which the correspondences are variable, inconsistent, sometimes arbitrary, and subject to lexical and morphological influences (English for example)`. (442) He argues that in shallow orthographies `it seems natural to teach reading by synthetic phonic methods `by which letters are decoded to sounds and then combined to form larger units such as syllables`. (442) In deep alphabetic orthographies, such as English, he argues for a `combined method by which children learn basic alphabetic

215

decoding procedures and at the same time master a `sight vocabulary` of familiar words` (442) He sets forth four levels for acquisition that he claims are applicable to all languages and orthographies, but claims the differences between languages influence the time needed to pass through a given phase and the linguistic units that are emphasised at each level. In his concluding remarks he points out that age of starting school and method of teaching in part determine the course of literacy acquisition, but:

> aspects of syllable structure and variations in orthographic depth, may be crucial in determining how the structures are formed and the amount of learning necessary for successful progression through each phase. (461)

In chapter 28, `Orthography, phonology and reading development: a cross-linguistic perspective`, Goswami claims that:

> Children come to the task of learning to read with varying degrees of phonological awareness, and so reading acquisition is never a purely `visual` task. However, as languages vary in their phonological structure and also in the consistency with which phonology is represented in orthography, cross-language differences in the development of certain aspects of lexical representation and in the development of phonological recoding strategies should be expected across orthographies. (Goswami, 2013: 463).

She states that it is simpler for children learning to read in consistent orthographies such as Italian, Spanish, Turkish, Greek and German and they seem to acquire reading at a faster rate than children learning to read in inconsistent orthographies such as English.

It seemed important to highlight issues such as these identified by Seymour and Goswami, as they make the level of discussions in England around learning to read appear somewhat simplistic when they fail to take account of the complexity of English orthography. This is also relevant in international comparisons of literacy, such as PIRLS and PISA (discussed in chapter 19).

Furthermore, figures released following a question in the House of Lords on 3 March 2014, revealed that by January 2013 19 per cent of pupils starting school in England in Year 1 had English as an additional language. (*Education Journal*, 2014, Issue 193: 23) The effect of this on literacy learning has received little attention in the debates. As noted in chapter 20, by 2011, at least half the world`s children learnt to read in their second language. (Deacon and Cain, 2011) This percentage is likely to increase.

Endnote

It is to be hoped that the issues discussed in this book will raise the level of debate around literacy learning and will show the relevance to both policy and practice of insights from research. The inclusion of illustrations both from children who learnt to read with little instruction, and at an early age, and of the continuing problems of older children and adults highlight some of the complexities of learning to be literate, in particular in a language such as English, with its deep orthography.

References

Balmuth, M. (1982) *The Roots of Phonics: a historical introduction.* McGraw Hill. A new edition of this book was published in 2009 with forewords by Jeanne Chall and Marilyn Adams.

Barr, J. E. (1985) *Understanding Children Spelling.* Edinburgh: The Scottish Council for Research in Education.

Bollmann, S. (2008) *Women who Read are Dangerous.* London: Merrill Publishers Ltd (English translation).

Clark, M. M. (1970) Reading *Difficulties in Schools.* Harmonsworth: Penguin.

Clark, M. M. (1976) *Young Fluent Readers: what can they teach us?* London: Heinemann.

Clark, M. M. Barr, J and McKee, F. (1982) *Pupils with Learning Difficulties in the Secondary School: progress and problems in developing a whole school policy.* Birmingham: University of Birmingham.

Crystal., D. (2012) *Spell it Out: the singular story of English spelling.* London: Profile Books.

Deacon, H and Cain, K. (2011) 'What have we learnt from learning to read in more than one language?' *Journal of Research in Reading,* 34 (1): 1-5.

Goswami, U. (2013) 'Orthography, phonology and reading development: a cross-linguistic perspective'. *In Handbook of Orthography and Literacy*, R. Malatesha Joshi and P .G. Aaron (eds). Chapter 28. New York: Routledge.

Kennedy, A. (1984) *The Psychology of Reading.* London: Methuen.

Malatesha Joshi, R and Aaron, P. G. (eds) (2013) *Handbook of Orthography and Literacy.* New York: Routledge.

Peters, M. L. (1967) *Spelling Caught or Taught?* London: Routledge and Kegan Paul.

Peters, M. L. (1970) *Success in Spelling.* Cambridge: Cambridge Institute of Education.

Read, C. (1986) *Children's Creative Spelling.* London: Routledge and Kegan Paul.

Seymour, P. H. K. (2013) 'Theoretical framework for beginning reading in different orthographies'. In *Handbook of Orthography and Literacy*, R. Malatesha Joshi and P.G. Aaron (eds). Chapter 27. New York: Routledge.

Seymour, P. H. K., Aro,, M. and Erskine, J. M. (2003) 'Foundation literacy acquisition in European orthographies', *British Journal of Psychology.* 94

Publications on Literacy by Margaret M. Clark: 1967 to 2014

Publications marked with an asterisk have been adapted for this book. The papers given at United Kingdom Reading Association conferences are listed separately, by date of publication.

Selected books on literacy

Clark, M. M. (1957) *Left-handedness: laterality characteristics and their educational implications*. London: University of London Press. Based on PhD, with studies of reading and writing difficulties.

Clark, M. M. (1974) *Teaching Left-handed Children*. London: Hodder and Stoughton. First edition 1959. Incidence figures, crossed laterality and writing difficulties discussed.

Clark, M. M. (1970) *Reading Difficulties in Schools*. Research funded by a grant from the Scottish Education Department. Harmondsworth: Penguin Books. New edition London: Heinemann Educational Books, 1979.

Clark, M. M. (1976) *Young Fluent Readers: what can they teach us?* Research funded by a grant from the Scottish Education Department. London: Heinemann Educational Books.

Clark, M. M. (1989) *Understanding Research in Early Education: the relevance for the future of lessons from the past*. London: Gordon and Breach. Second Edition, 2005. London: Routledge. Section IV What can we learn from children who succeed is an analysis of two of my major funded researches on literacy. This part was also published in Danish in a journal.

*Clark, M. M. (1994) *Young Literacy Learners: how can we help them*. Leamington Spa: Scholastic.

*Clark, M. M., Barr, J. and McKee, F. (1982) *Pupils with Learning Difficulties in the Secondary School: progress and problems in developing a* *whole-school policy*. Final Report of a Scottish Education Department funded project. Birmingham: Faculty of Education.

Clark, M. M. and Dewhirst, W. (1986-88) *Time for a Story*, a television series for children of four to six years of age. We were consultants and wrote the teachers' booklets. Manchester: Granada Television.

*Clark, M.M. (1995) *Language Learning and the Urban Child.* Self-published.

Selected edited books, with a chapter or chapters as author

*Clark, M. M. and Cheyne, W. M. (eds) (1979) *Studies in Pre-school Education.* London: Hodder and Stoughton. Reference to studies by C. Lomax from chapter 6 and W. Donachy from section III.

Clark, M. M. and Glynn, T. (eds) (1980) *Reading and Writing for the Child with Difficulties.* Educational Review. Occ. Pub. No 8. Birmingham: University of Birmingham.

Clark, M. M. (ed) (1985) *New Directions in the Study of Reading.* London: Falmer Press.

*Clark, M. M. and Munn, P. (eds) (1997) *Education in Scotland: policy and practice from pre-school to secondary.* London: Routledge. From chapters 1, 3 and 7.

Selected articles and chapters in books

*Clark, M. M. (1975) `Language and reading; research trends' in *Problems of Language and Learning,* A. Davies, (ed). London; Heinemann Educational in association with SSCR and SsRE. This is a report of a seminar in Edinburgh in 1973 with in addition papers by M.A.K. Halliday on Sociolinguistics; dialect by H. H. Speitel; Psychology by J. S. Bruner; Teaching of writing by J. Briton and chaired by B. Bernstein. Participants also included Marie Clay, Margaret Donaldson, Jessie Reid and Joan Tough.

*Clark, M. M. (1982) `What can we learn from them? A comparison of the strengths and weaknesses of young fluent readers and children with reading difficulties`. In *Reading, Writing and Multiculturalism,* D. Barnes, A. Campbell and R. Jones (eds). 96-103. Plenary papers from Australian Reading Association Conference. Adelaide: Australian Reading Association.

Clark, M. M. (1983) `Reading: trends in teaching and learning`. In *Nuevas Perspectivas en Psicologia del Desarrollo en Lengua Inglesa,* H. R. Schaffer (ed); 185-200. Madrid: Grafisa. Only published in Spanish.

*Clark, M. M. (1984) `Literacy at home and at school`. In *Awakening to Literacy,* H. Goelman, A. Oberg and F. Smith (eds): 122-130. Exeter, New Hampshire: Heinemann Educational.

Clark, M. M. (1986) `Educational technology and children with moderate learning difficulties`, *The Exceptional Child* Vol. 33. No. 1: 28-34. Based on paper given at the Concerned Technology in Education International Conference in Edinburgh in 1985. Also published in Danish.

Clark M. M. (1988a) *Reading Revised: 21 years of reading research.* Paper delivered at award of SCRE Fellowship for outstanding contribution to Educational Research. SCRE publication 101. Edinburgh: SCRE.

*Clark, M. M. (1988b) `Literacy learning in creative contexts`. In *Children's Creative Communication* in R. Söderbergh (ed). Plenary papers from Fourth International Congress for the Study of Child Language. Lund 1987: 103-109. Lund: Lund University Press.

Clark, M. M. (1992) `Sensitive observation and the development of literacy`, *Educational Psychology.* Vol. 12 Nos 3 and 4: 215-223. The issue was on Early Literacy Learning: a tribute to Marie Clay.

Clark, M. M. (1998) `Electronic books`. *The Author.* Spring: 27-28.

*Clark, M. M. (2003) `International studies of reading, such as PIRLS – a cautionary tale`, *Education Journal.* Issue 75: 25-27.

*Clark, M. M. (2006) `The Rose Report in context: what will be its impact on the teaching of reading?` *Educational Journal.* Issue 97: 27-29.

*Clark, M. M. (2012a) `Literacies in and for a changing world: what is the evidence?` In C. Clouder, B. Heys, M. Matthes M., and P. Sullivan (eds) *Improving the Quality of Childhood in Europe 2012*. Chapter 5. Vol.3. East Sussex: European Council for Steiner Waldorf Education. www.ecswe.com/publication-qoc-europe-2012php.

Clark, M. M. (2012b) `Literacy teaching – from government policy to classroom practice`. *Race, Equality Teaching.* Vol. 31 (1): 11-13.

*Clark, M. M. (2013a) `Is there one best method of teaching reading? What is the evidence?` *Education Journal.* Issue 156 March: 14-16.

*Clark, M. M. (2013b) `The phonics check for all Year 1 children in England: its background, results and possible effects`. *Education Journal.* Issue 160 April: 6-8.

*Clark, M. M. (2013c) `Research evidence on the first phonics check for all Year 1 children in England: is it accurate and is it necessary?` *Education Journal.* Issue 168 June: 12-15.

Clark, M. M. (2013d) `From literacy research to government policy and classroom practice in the early years: what is the evidence?` In *From Literacy Research to Classroom Practice: Insights and Inspiration,* Proceedings of the 2012 Annual Conference of the Reading Association of Ireland. Dublin: RAI: 32-39.

*Clark, M. M. (2013e) High frequency words: a neglected resource for young literacy learners. *Reading News,* Autumn 2013: 15-17.

*Clark, M.M. (2013f) The phonics check for Year 1 children in England: unresolved issues of its value and validity after two years. *Education Journal.* Issue 177. October: 13-15.

*Clark, M. M. (2014a) `Whose knowledge counts in Government literacy policies and at what cost?` *Education Journal* Issue 188:13-16.

*Clark, M. M. (2014b) ` The impact of an IMPACT pamphlet: on decoding synthetic phonics`. *Education Journal* Issue 188: 12-13.

Papers at UKRA conferences, by date of publication in proceedings: papers given 1966 and 1991.

1967 Clark, M. M. `The use of television with backward readers in the Glasgow area`. In *Reading: Current Research and Practice* Vol. One, A. Brown (ed). 24-32. Edinburgh: Chambers. Paper delivered at 3rd conference in Cambridge in 1966 reprinted in the following:

1972 Clark, M. M. `The use of television with backward readers in the Glasgow area` in 1972. In *The First R: yesterday today and tomorrow,* J. Morris (ed). 162-168. London: Ward Lock Educational. See above.

1972 Clark M. M. `Training the teachers of reading (report of a working group), 185-190 and Reading difficulties in schools`: 213-218. In *Literacy at all Levels*, V. Southgate (ed). London: Ward Lock Educational. Given at 8th conference in Manchester in1971.

*1973 Clark M. M. `Reading and related skills`, (presidential address). In *Reading and Related Skills,* M. M. Clark and A. Milne (eds): 3-13. London: Ward Lock Educational. Given at 9th conference in 1972 in Hamilton.

1975 Clark M. M. `Language and reading: a study of early reading`. In *The Road to Effective Reading,* W. Latham (ed). 17-26. London: Ward Lock Educational. Given at 10th conference in Totley-Thorbridge in 1973.

1977 Clark M. M. `The realities of remedial reading`. In *Reading Research and Classroom Practice,* J. Gilliland (ed): 37-43. London: Ward Lock Educational. Given at 13th conference in 1976 in Durham.

1988 Clark M. M. `New directions in the study of reading`. In *Reading the abc and Beyond,* C. Anderson (ed): 176-182. Basingstoke: Macmillan Education. Given at 24th conference in Edinburgh.

1992 Clark M. M. `Reading in 1990s: a spring forward or a fall back?` In *Literacy Without Frontiers*, F. Satow and B. Gatherer (eds). 30-38. Widnes, Cheshire: UKRA. Given at 28th conference in 1991.

Endorsements

The following endorsements, and those on the back cover, have been written by professional colleagues who have read a pre-publication draft of the book. I am grateful to them for taking the time to read and comment on such online material.

This book is a remarkable account of how we should approach teaching `learning to be literate` in an age when we are increasingly told by Government both what we should teach and how we should teach it. It is a must read story of research and practice, drawing on a wonderful wealth of experience in the development of reading. We are reminded all too clearly in this approach to educational research of the teacher as expert professional and of one who should aspire to be both a `reflective` and `thinking` practitioner. Professor Stephen Rayner, Dean of Education, Newman University, Birmingham.

This exceptional book documents and critically analyses literacy education over a period of fifty years. Margaret Clark continues in her relentless quest to raise awareness of the changing nature and quality of literacy research evidence, theory and practice. Her goal has ever been to ensure that the best evidence underpins literacy education policy. She rightly draws attention to the complexity of the orthographic, syntactic and semantic processes a young reader must master in order to make sense of written text, and the danger in any government policy that stresses one best method. The author sets out to dispel `a few myths`. In so doing, she assures her position among the most influential figures in literacy research of her generation. Carol Aubrey, a former student of the author and now Professor Emeritus, Warwick University.

Name Index

*Because of the nature of this book, references to publications by the author are to be found in most chapters. However, in this index reference is made only to the chapters where my research is considered in detail.

228